PASSING

PASSING

A Strategy to Dissolve Identities and Remap Differences

Anna Camaiti Hostert

Translated from the Italian Version
by Christine Marciasini

Madison • Teaneck
Fairleigh Dickinson University Press

Associated University Presses
2010 Eastpark Boulevard
Cranbury, NJ 08512

The paper used in this publication meets the requirements of the American National Standard for Permanence of Paper for Printed Library Materials Z39.48-1984.

Library of Congress Cataloging-in-Publication Data

Camaiti Hostert, Anna.
[Passing. English]
Passing : a strategy to dissolve identities and remap differences / Anna Camaiti Hostert ; translated from the Italian version by Christine Marciasini.
p. cm.
Includes bibliographical references (p.) and index.
ISBN-13: 978-0-8386-4125-5 (alk. paper)
ISBN-10: 0-8386-4125-3 (alk. paper)
1. Self (Philosophy) 2. Passing (Identity) 3. Identity (Psychology) I. Title.
BD450.C23713 2007
302′.1—dc22

2007010695

PRINTED IN THE UNITED STATES OF AMERICA

Dark Times . . . are not identical with the monstrosities of this century which indeed are of a horrible novelty. Dark times . . . are no rarity in history, although they were perhaps unknown in American history, which otherwise has its fair share, past and present, of crime and disaster. [E]ven in the darkest of times we have the right to expect some illumination, and such illumination may well come less from theories and concepts than from the uncertain, flickering, and often weak light that some men and women, in their lives and their works, will kindle under almost all circumstances and shed over the time span that was given them on earth [. . .]. Eyes so used to darkness as ours will hardly be able to tell whether their light was the light of a candle or that of a blazing sun. But such objective evaluation . . . can safely be left to posterity.

—Hannah Arendt, *Men in Dark Times*

Contents

Preface to the English Version

IN THIS PREFACE TO THE ENGLISH VERSION OF *PASSING: DISSOLVING IDENTITIES, Overcoming Differences*, I want to situate the notion of passing within analytical and theoretical space if for no other reason than to alert the reader to my recognition of the highly emotionally charged, contested, and problematic history of the peculiar social phenomenon and literary trope of passing. Indeed, at the risk of losing, in "translation," certain intuitive and even inexpressible insights, it seems that whatever surplus of meaning that resists theoretical exhaustion, I must at least insist on taking seriously my ethical obligation to assume responsibility for the other. I must assume this responsibility in order to avoid seeking a diminution of the other to the same in my efforts to transport passing from its familiar context within the African American literary tradition to other sites of contestation. Here, I want to issue a caution. In seeking to migrate the notion of passing from its familiar context of racial passing to other sites of contestation, I acknowledge the risks and opportunities of such an undertaking. However, I do not seek to erase the singularity of the dynamics of race and racism for the sake of any reductionism that invites us to treat all passing as the same. Certainly, the cruel history of racial oppression in the American context and modernity's involvement in the instituting of a racial mode of consciousness require an "infinite" vigilance in resisting false boundaries of racial inclusion and exclusion.

In borrowing the notion of passing from the African American context, I refuse the temptation to engage in any project of reverse semantic, meaning attempting to redefine passing and then argue for a rereading/rewriting of history from the conceptual frame of a new understanding of passing. Rather, it is my contention that the African American tradition can provide us not only with biographical materials but also with theoretical resources to construct different readings and interpretations. Hence, I will extend the notion of passing, not with the intent of necessarily changing it but, rather, to exploit its cognitive potency as a category of analysis. I will offer some general foundational remarks about passing, but not a necessary and sufficient definition of the term. Second, I will review the traditional interpretation of passing. After I do this, I will explore some recent interpretations of passing and conclude with a description of my own intended use of the notion of passing.

General Remarks

Like so many other concepts, passing is an essentially contested notion. There is no general definition of it that will receive universal endorsement. Samira Kawash has indicated that the verb form of the Latin passus means to "to step, pace, [and] walk." She further maintains that by the eleventh century a change occurred, and it now designated movement "from place to place."[1]

Of course the semantic indeterminacy regarding "passing" can be tamed once we specify a context of use; and it is precisely through this semantic weaving that the notion of passing acquires its appropriate meanings. The theoretical density of passing has not escaped all scholars. Juda Bennet describes passing as a "literary device, a philosophical conundrum, and a historical phenomenon."[2] Nevertheless, it bears noting that there seems to be an isomorphic relation between the semantic unruliness of passing and its own material effects in the world. Passing creates social chaos precisely because it involves the undermining of a rigid system of racial classification. Passing disrupts a social and political order grounded on the expectation of the existence of two distinctive races and, hence, the act of a light-skinned black passing for white is to invite ontological, metaphysical and semantic chaos—race becomes unstable, the world seems to escape categorical discipline, and language loses its capacity to transmit meaning.

Due to the cruel social, political, cultural, and historical realities of the system of racial oppression characteristic of American society, passing assumed a peculiar role relative to the African American situation. For whites, passing (the idea of whites becoming black) was not an existential option for them simply because the idea of such a transformation was far beyond their imagination. As Edmund Morgan has argued, no matter how poor whites were, the one thing they valued in common was the fact of not being black.[3]

Since light-skinned blacks could pass for whites, the social phenomenon of passing, and passing as a literary trope, took on great significance for African Americans. Maria Fabi has suggested that the trope of passing or, rather, passing as a root metaphor, serves as the foundation of the

African-American novelistic tradition. She writes, In *Passing and the Rise of the African American Novel* I argue the distinctiveness of the poetic of passing in pre-Harlem Renaissance fiction, demonstrating its centrality to the rise and development of the African American novelistic tradition."[4]

In attributing transcendental status to passing, it is important to mention the impotence of positivist and empiricist modes of analysis in the study of this phenomenon. If we operate with the idea of passing as a social phenomenon, then it would seem that we should be able to study it. We should be able to obtain knowledge about the individuals who choose to pass, their reasons for passing, and how passing has changed them both psychologically and culturally. But just as passing invites social and political chaos, it also invites epistemological chaos. Passing exposes the limits of racial epistemology, as well as the poverty of empiricist epistemologies. The most obvious social scientific, hence empiricist, approach to passing comes from Gunnar Myrdal. He defines passing as follows: "For all practical purposes 'passing' means that a Negro becomes a white man, that is, moves from the lower to the higher caste. In the American caste order, this can be accomplished only by the deception of the white people with whom the passer comes to associate and by a conspiracy of silence on the part of other Negroes who might know about it."[5] Myrdal clearly offers us a commonsense understanding of passing, passing as deception in which a black becomes white and thereby earns social promotion. Later, I will examine other approaches that transcend this commonsense understanding of passing. However, at this time, it is interesting to note that the very conditions of passing render passing epistemologically opaque to empiricist epistemologies. With any rigid binary and hierarchical structure, there are two classes of people, the privileged and the marginalized. If such a system is a racial system of classification, passing becomes a possibility, but "the very condition of possibility for passing is secrecy."[6] Since secrecy is the condition of possibility for passing, it would seem that passing is beyond the regime of empirical study. To reveal oneself as passing is the possibility of the impossibility of continuing to pass. So, if the revelation of passing is to make passing no longer possible, then the empirical study of passing becomes difficult, if not impossible. James Conyers, in his efforts to write a sociology of passing, states that "In view of the scanty data available concerning the practice of passing in the United States, it is not possible to state with any degree of certainty what the consequences of this practice have been."[7] Before Conyers, Louis Wirth and Herbert Goldhamer lamented the difficulty of studying passing precisely because of the conditions of its possibility, namely, secrecy. However, the limitations of empiricism should not lead us to mistakenly conclude that "passing is the fictitious creation of novelists."[8] Rather, passing lends itself to the kind of literate imagination characteristic of literary production, namely, narratives and autobiographies.

Traditional Approach to Passing

Let us briefly examine the traditional approach to passing. Clearly, the institutionalized view has been to see passing as a negation of subjectivity, read as the denial of one's essential racial self. Hence, on this view, passing is the intentional presenting of oneself to the world in a manner that conflicts with how the individual in question views himself or herself. One sees oneself in a certain way yet deceptively presents oneself in a manner contradictory to that vision. Passing is to present oneself as something that one is not; it is a matter of violating the laws of identity and sameness. In so viewing passing as deception, as an individual assuming a counterfeit identity, the tendency has been to understand passing as racial self-hatred. Although we would not want to deny that some individuals suffer from self–hatred, the tendency to uncritically scrutinize passing as obvious self-hatred links passing within the pejorative tradition of withholding human agency from African Americans[9] and preferring to view them as victims. There is no exaggeration in holding that the traditional approach to passing was primarily psychological in orientation, seen as the manifestation of deep fractures in the psyches of those who engaged in passing. The character of the tragic mulatto is the paradigmatic model of this conception of passing. As Phillip Harper maintains, racial passing has been seen "in psychic-orientational terms, as signifying only the protagonist's disavowal of an identity that proper race pride and healthy self-regard would lead him or her enthusiastically to embrace."[10]

Passing and Ontology

Before jumping into the more recent approaches to passing, I think that it would be most helpful to examine some of the ontological implications of passing. First, it bears noting that there is a certain language or semantic of passing: passing as being an impostor, as being a fake, as being an infiltrator, as being opportunistic, as pretending, as concealing, and as simulating. This semantic of passing operates in accordance with a logic grounded in a reality and appearance distinction. Hence, passing is a matter of taking the appearance for the reality.

There is also a certain ontological asymmetry regarding passing. According to the one-drop rule, in order to be white all of one's ancestors must be white. However, to be black requires only that one have a single drop of black blood in one's ancestry. One drop of black blood makes an individual black, but it is not the case that one drop of white blood makes an individual white. Whiteness is purity of blood, whereas blackness, ontologically speaking, admits to no absolute purity of blood. So we see that passing, understood as a black passing for white, is ontologically a paradox, for it requires that "the thing is what it is not, and is not what it is."[11] Passing, furthermore, is ontologically perverted precisely because it involves substituting illusion for reality and perception for knowledge.

New Approaches to Passing

With the preceding context in place, a critical review of recent approaches to passing is in order. Samira Kawash views passing as pregnant with significant epistemological implications. She maintains that "passing challenges the principles and the power of [our] racial epistemology."[12] Passing is epistemologically disruptive precisely because it calls into question the epistemology of race grounded in the visibility of sign and image, what Linda Schlossberg has called the "logic of visibility."[13] If knowledge of blackness and its essence is dependent upon certain visible signs, passing disrupts this epistemological regime to the extent that it accommodates blacks passing for whites. To this extent, as earlier mentioned, passing brings about the uncertainty of whiteness, for if a black can pass for white, the issue then becomes what to make of whiteness. In line with her new approach to passing, Kawash argues that Johnson's *The Autobiography of an Ex-Coloured Man* and Nella Larsen's *Passing* are not token texts denouncing racial passing but rather are texts that unsettle established understandings of racial identity and racial knowledge.[14]

Kathleen Pfeiffer has provocatively maintained that passing should be seen as part of American individualism, the tradition in which individuals make and remake themselves. According to her, we need not limit passing only to the idea of a disconnection between an individual's inner black self and his or her outer white self. She writes that "Few critics have even noted the echoes of individualism that reverberate in race passing, and none have examined those echoes as fully as I do here. Many commentators have considered the degree to which passing narratives grow out of distinctively African American traditions; but as I demonstrate, those are counterbalanced by their simultaneous reflection of intellectual traditions that have generally been defined as canonical."[15] So, in Pfeiffer's view, passing is part of the noble tradition of self-making, the tradition of the expression of human agency and subjectivity and not, as commonly claimed, a denial of self. Pfeiffer's thesis on passing is best summarized in her own words and deserves a long quotation: Must passing necessarily indicate a denial of 'blackness,' or racial self-hatred and nothing more? [I] propose that when we look at the passer as a figure who values individualism, who may be idiosyncratic, self-determining, or inclined toward improvisation, we invite a much richer and more complex reading. Moreover, when we recognize that the passer often demonstrates ambivalence about whiteness as well as blackness, we avail ourselves of the passing figure's more complicated nuances.[16]

Werner Sollors has similarly framed passing outside the narrow frame of racial self-hatred. He prefers to view passing as situated in the structural conflict between identity as achieved and identity as ascribed. In so locating passing, Sollors intends to complicate our understanding of passing. According to him, "The paradoxical coexistence of the cult of the social upstart as 'self-made man' and the permanent racial identification and moral condemnation of the racial passer as 'imposter,' constitute the frame within which the phenomenon of passing took place."[17]

Gayle Wald in *Crossing the Line: Racial Passing in Twentieth-Century U.S. Literature and Culture,* to some extent remains within the traditional paradigm of viewing "the enterprise of passing to be contradictory, self-defeating, or otherwise impracticable."[18] But she adds a new twist to the debate about passing when she claims that narratives of passing pose an ethical/political challenge to contemporary readers. Narratives of passing "ask contemporary readers to consider their own political, theoretical, or ideological interests in race as a site of identification and political or cultural investment, its fictional qualities notwithstanding."[19]

Unlike Wald, Cheryl Wall has courageously chosen to break with tradition and approaches passing narratives as being about gender and not exclusively about race. Wall maintains that "In Larsen's novel [Passing], 'passing' does not refer only to the sociological phenomenon of blacks crossing the color line. It represents instead both the loss of racial identity and the denial of self required of women who conform to restrictive gender roles."[20] Wall further extends her analysis of passing, choosing to read it as "a metaphor of death and desperation . . . supported by images of asphyxiation, suffocation, and claustrophobia."[21]

Passing and Fictions of Identity, edited by Elaine Ginsberg, is perhaps the most recent popular text on passing. Ginsberg in the introduction reads passing as a challenge to essentialism, while underscoring the construction of identity. The fact that identities are constructed places them beyond the modalities of truth and falsity. According to her, "For both the process and the discourse of passing challenges the essentialism that is often the foundation of identity politics, a challenge that may be seen as either threatening or liberating but in either instance discloses the truth that identities are not singularly true or false but multiple and contingent."[22] The common theme characteristic of these new interpretations of passing is the idea of extending passing beyond the context of race.

Transgressing Canonical Boundaries of Passing

As for my own take on passing, I follow in the approach hinted at by Ginsberg and the others who seek to link passing with postmodernist sentiments. I propose treating passing as a metaphor for identity formation, as well as a metaphor of transgression—for the practice of violating boundaries that masquerade as absolute and universal when they are, in fact, contingent, historical, and local. In so framing passing as a metaphor of subjectivity, namely, as the act of one creating or choosing an identity, I extend passing beyond its customary racial context and view it as applicable to situation where the politics of identity are always at work. Charles Scruggs's description of Ginsberg's edited volume captures the spirit of my position. Scruggs writes that the text frames passing "as a metaphor for the postmodernist enterprise of understanding the coherence of identity. Indeed, the two words . . . 'destabilize' and 'imbricate,' imply that the protean self not only may 'pass' for white or black, male or female, homosexual or heterosexual, foreign or native, but may experience ever-shifting permutations of these fictional identities."[23] In framing passing as metaphor, I also want to suggest that passing can function as an analytical category that would apply, for example, to women passing for men, and lesbians and gays passing as straight. There is also the possibility of exporting passing to works of literature in which fiction would pass as autobiography. And there is also the social world of power, the context where power differentials are always in play. To the extent "that dominant groups use, or even create, 'others' in order to identify themselves, passing, then, threatens the dominant group, not only by allowing people of the other group into one's own but also by calling into question the whole group's identity."[24] Passing can be used to remind us of the contingency of our institutions and how structures of feelings are not discovered but are invented to include as well as to exclude.

Consistent with my position, Pamela Caughie has also reworked passing as metaphor within a postmodernist frame. From a postmodernist perspective, passing adequately qualifies to assist in theorizing identity beyond the confines of essentialism and fixity. Caughie maintains that "all subjectivity is passing."[25] Clearly she does not mean to suggest that all subjectivity is fake or unreal but, rather, is a matter of presentation of self. Such presentation cannot always be the same and will accordingly change to accommodate shifting and contradictory situations. Passing offers the possibility of working oneself from within historically inherited identities to fashion identities of our own choosing. Accordingly, I also view passing as a refusal to be confined within historically limiting structures of existence. But just as passing is a refusal of the given, it is also an opportunity of renewal and growth.

Finally, in breaking with the commonsense notion of passing as the presenting of a false self in place of a true self, as a substitution of appearance for reality, my postmodernist appropriation of passing views passing as not a mere inversion of the reality and appearance distinction but, rather, as transcending this either/or choice, the choice of the self as real or the self as appearance. In its new context, passing repudiates all efforts to ground intelligibility and identity in a transcendental signified. It invites us to acknowledge that the privileged terms of the metaphysics of presence do not and cannot designate substantial realities that claim our unconditional allegiance. In ending, I share Kawash's view that "Unlike the cultural logic of passing defined as a deception opposed to the true identity hiding underneath appearance . . . there is no authentic, original identity that could be hidden or imitated; there are only copies and copies of copies that give the impression of originality."[26] Passing, far from instigating denial of one's true self, perhaps offers the most readily available process to acquire a notion of self, even if we cannot claim an essential self.

For this preface I am indebted to Clevis Headley, Professor of Philosophy and Director of Ethnic Studies at Florida Atlantic University. We discussed extensively the notion of passing and he gave me inputs, which were precious. I want to thank him for helping me not only in writing this introduction, but also in the difficult journey of understanding my own self better.

Acknowledgments

I WROTE THIS BOOK ORIGINALLY BECAUSE MY PERSONAL EXPERIENCE AND my scholarly work have prompted me to redefine my own identity and my own self. The African American practice of *passing* has taught me, on the one hand, how painful and difficult it is to live the condition of not being accepted for who we are. On the other hand, it has also showed me how living *in between* cultures and ethnic backgrounds can carry with it an innovative and relative point of view which is at the core of any *transnational* and *transcultural* identity.

This book was originally published in Italy in 1996 under the title of *Passing. Dissolvere le identità, superare le differenze* and it has been republished in 2006 with the same title by a different Italian publisher.

The publication in English has required additional editing work and an additional Preface for which I am deeply indebted to Clevis Headley, professor of Philosophy and Director of Ethnic Studies at Florida Atlantic University without whom I could not have written it.

In addition, I would like to express my sincere gratitude to Anthony Julian Tamburri, Dean of the Calandra Institute for his encouraging suggestions and for his long time friendship. I am also grateful to professor Harry Keyishian of Farleigh Dickinson University Press, whose help was instrumental in reviewing some parts of the book for the English version. I want to thank both of them for their precious ideas and Marina Banchetti, Chair of the Philosophy Department for having read with me the last draft of the manuscript.

A special thanks goes to Tricia Amiel who substantially assisted me in editing the book. Her suggestions and her professional, attentive help were very precious to me and to the final version of the book.

I am also grateful to Julien Yoseloff, Christine Retz, and all the people at the Associated University Presses who were very patient and followed step by step the editing of this book.

Finally, last, but most definitely not least, I want to express my deep, affectionate gratitude to my husband George for being present in all the phases of this book, from the Italian versions to the publication in English, and for being always supportive during the course of this long journey.

Introduction

THE *THAWING SEASON* WAS THE NAME GIVEN IN THE SOVIET UNION TO the post-Stalinist period of political and cultural dissension. This period seemed destined to open democratic fissures in societies imprisoned in the icy grip of Marxist-Leninist ideology, until then perceived as relentless and immutable. Packed under this frozen political surface were individuals, social groups, ethnic, and religious identities. These were often in contrast among themselves, moving restlessly in confined spaces and within limited environments, struggling against the restrictions on freedom of speech, freedom of action, and freedom of movement. Unfortunately, this *coupure* turned out to be only a small rent in the ideological web, and not only was it incapable of melting the frozen curtain that enveloped the socialist systems, but, in fact, it turned out to be a first, desperately unequivocal sign that the expression "socialism with a human face" was a contradiction in terms. The Communist utopia, of which those regimes were believed to represent a transitory phase, was already showing the first signs of the malaise from which it was never to recover. Future developments in all Socialist countries world-wide—coupled with feminist, libertarian, pacifist, and anti-authoritarian movements in the industrialized West at the end of the sixties that rebelled against that mentality—have proven that this fragility was not the consequence of a deviation from original "good" premises but was embedded in the basic structure of the original political project. At the end of the eighties, Socialist regimes in eastern countries melted like snow in August, collapsing under the weight of the inability to transform themselves. Their disappearance made orphans of an entire generation of Western Communists. Meanwhile, within their borders enormous human masses have lost their cultural bearings and, on the one hand, are ready to fight to reestablish their personal freedom, as well as their social and ethnic identities and, on the other, to pour beyond the banks of their native countries like a giant flood, urged on by the will to survive and the long-suppressed anger of the oppressed.

Living in a cold city close to Lake Michigan makes it possible for me, when winter hardens the surface of this enormous liquid mass into a thick layer of ice, to listen to a dull murmuring, the sound of the waters trapped underneath awaiting spring to resurface. One is impressed by the low rumbling of hidden currents, the more so because this turbulence is in marked contrast with the image of stasis offered by the icy lid that confines their liquidity, and the impression is truly that of a live being struggling to escape suffocation. If the leaders of the Communist nomenklature, especially of the Soviet Union, had realized the sense of oppression their static, unbending regimes produced and the risk they were running in their pursuit of a blind, antilibertarian totalitarianism, they probably would have built party schools close to rivers in Siberia rather than reserving the area for dissidents.

The transition from winter to spring, the *thawing season,* the moment of the transformation from solid to liquid, is the process I am describing in this book. What I wish to do is bring to the dangerous but fascinating surface of nonterritorial waters those aspects of our individual and social selves that have been suffocated under the ice of world-views and repressive narrative forms. Now, in conjunction with the technological revolution of the digital era, they have the opportunity to resume their liquid form. The metaphor of liquidity recalls the image of mixing bodily fluids, accused of being the main cause of the transmission of AIDS, and with it the image of the body as a fabricated entity that is banished from the realm of social communication. The substance of personal relations has been impoverished and sterilized and has lost the subversive potential created by the immediacy of sensuality and desire, quenched in the formality of aseptic intercourse devoid of physicality. But AIDS, by striking especially against homosexuals and heroine-addicts, also brought to light individuals whom the heterosexual and moralistic narrative and social contract had always repressed and hidden, as deviations from the "natural" norms of society. Thus, the already irreversible crisis of the traditional concept of subjectivity was compounded by disquieting forms of alternative expression, aggravating the precariousness of a model of rationality that had long been perceived as necessary and natural. Previously, concepts such as "order and harmony" had seemed embedded in reality; they were much more than concepts, since, in a gigantic shift from thought to reality and being, they were transformed into the most hard and enduring ontological structures. "Thus reason (or more precisely a specific form of reason) appeared as a super order, as an absolute cosmic harmony and, at the same time, as the *natural* disciplinary norm of the mind. The human eye does not open on the original darkness of the world but on the scene of a cosmos already illuminated by the light of the intellect."[1] Within this model of reason the concepts of identity (whether ethnic, racial, religious, or sexual), of conscience and of subjectivity play a fundamental role, and the consequences of this change, analyzed at length in the postmodern debate, inevitably refer to their more systematic construction performed by modernity, and by Hegelian modernity in particular.

Let's Spit on Hegel was the bold suggestion contained in a small pamphlet published by Carla Lonzi in 1970. I have always liked that impertinent and ironic title, which invited contempt for one of the founding fathers of idealism, who had had so much influence on Marxian thought, and for this reason, during those years, was usually thought of with great respect. Lonzi attacked the ideological tenets of the patriarchal and bourgeois universe that were at the core of Hegel's philosophy, providing the basis for the omnivorous system of historical-dialectic thought and of a seamless subjectivity. More specifically, Lonzi focused her attention on the *Phenomenology of Spirit* and on the slave-master relationship that serves as its guiding principle. This relationship, thanks to its capacity to subsume within the principle of rationality and therefore of reality the man-woman relationship, prevents the latter from being inscribed in the human-social realm. While the master-slave relationship is a relation between men on which all social coexistence and dialectics are based, the man-woman relationship may be construed as a stable and natural datum, centered on a sexual essentialism and a hierarchical structure with man at the top and woman at the bottom. But revolutionary Marxian dialectics is also based on the slave-master dialectic, for while it has criticized and subverted the bourgeois connotations of Hegel's position, it has maintained intact its theoretical structure, without altering "social roles" and without "a substantial change in values." "The communist revolution," writes Lonzi, "was based on male political and cultural values *and on the repression and instrumentalization of feminism* and is now confronted with the revolt against male values that women intend to carry to the end, beyond the dialectics of class that occur within the confines of the patriarchal system."[2] There was reason to be angry, because the great majority of revolutionary "comrades" showed no intention of criticizing patriarchal authority, on which the certitude and "naturalness" of sexual contract was based. But in order for disregard towards the systematic Leviathan to be more than skin-deep, in order for it to hook its nails into the flesh of this monstrous vampire of Western modernity, it is necessary to pierce its genetic background. This is what Carla Lonzi did early on, for example when advocating the need to resist the ideological temptation of negating the subversive potential of the hippie movements of the sixties. Precisely in their being described by Marxian narratives as "non dialectical moments" of society and in their "abandoning the culture of the seizure of power and the political models adopted by male-dominated groups,"[3] Lonzi saw evidence of a reconciliation of public and private and a capacity for mediation that excluded a priori the synthesis of power.

From our perspective, however, this concept of "mediation" of Hegelian origin must necessarily be subject to a critique, notwithstanding Lonzi's efforts to femininize it or purify it of the desire for power. Even when one tries to liberate it from the circular, totalizing process that erases all contradictions between things and words, this concept inevitably runs the risk of reproposing forms of dominion, since it remains a more or less legitimate child of the idea of reason that generated it and shares its same genetic code. It can neither be made to rest like Sleeping Beauty waiting to be roused by the kiss of a generically "new" type of politics nor be modified into a female form of mediation, which, even if based on the distinction between "authority and power," as in Hannah Arendt, is not a guarantee against the risk of excessively rigid and structured relations of domination.

What the most radical wings of the hippie and feminist movements sought was the influence of the personal sphere (of more intimate desires and needs) over the public sphere, i.e., rather than the seizure of the Winter Palace. The most "revolutionary" characteristic of these movements was not the idea of alternative mediations so much as the ability to withdraw from the dominant cultural and narrative models that tended to relegate them to marginal and absolutely legible identities.

The most subversive action of these movements was, therefore, to bring to light personal desires in opposition to the single, visible perspective of all forms of political mediations: the seizure of power. In Italy, feminism was responsible for bringing this issue to the foreground. It is not surprising that the debate was extremely heated, since it centered on a sore spot of patriarchal politics: the separation of the private and public spheres. *Personal is political* went a famous Italian feminist slogan of the seventies. It criticized the fact that the private sphere was ignored in favor of an omnivorous political view that sought to make the process of transformation completely transparent and public, without altering in the least the structure of the family or the view of sexuality on which the change was based. The personal experiences of women, which were the result of a social and cultural system that relegated them to the private sphere, became the subject of a political debate that highlighted the extent to which in Italy both the historical and the extraparliamentary Left were dominated by traditional patriarchal culture. Feminist and student movements in Western countries helped engender the crisis of male subjectivity and consequently of the cultural model of reason on which it was based, bringing to light new subjects, new social relations, and new narratives. It is therefore with the same gaze of Benjamin's angel of history, turned upon these cultural and political mutant embryos we are experiencing, that I wish to approach the future. The libertarian, anarchic, and communitarian spirit of the American hippie movement of the sixties, the first manifestation, artistic more than political, of the European 1968 students' riots in Paris, and the feminist movement, with its critique of the cultural model of disparity between men and women, all marked a process of epochal transformation in the structure of social and political relations. They also foretold a path that is already visible in some aspects of the technological revolution we are currently undergoing and that will increasingly modify our everyday life and our way of communicating. All this has changed our notion of belonging and of social relations, forcing a reevaluation of the notion of a community independent of permanent ties and the territorialization of the other and of the self. The way we position ourselves is the result of choices dictated by desire, not by power relations based on stable identities, whether of nationality, race, religion, or sex.

It was during the sixties that people began discussing nonstructured, leaderless, communitarian moments in which the selective and centralized authority of information was no less an enemy than the bourgeois state. It was during this period that subjectivities, like that of women, which had been repressed for so long, began to play a role in history, demonstrating an agility and flexibility that are essential to current "infospheric" communicative relations. There is a need for new ideas and new words to describe the changes we are undergoing. The protean and flexible disposition of those distant, communitarian, social, and political moments helps us think anew, elaborating original concepts suitable to this era of transition. *Passing* is one of these concepts. Yet, nothing is invented that did not already exist, and all that this concept does is to make visible fluid states that were previously suppressed. Writes Bifo:

> Concepts are not democratic, they are not born out of an agreement but create a path, giving direction to a tendency. Either they work or they do not work. If they work they open a small window, they send rays of light on an

> object in formation, which can be now seen, as it never was seen before. And concepts are also words, sounds, emotions, fears, and hopes. Thinking new words, words that reunite different ascendancies and alternative imaginations is a way to discover or rather to construct real objects, which can be communicated and modified. All this neologistic activity to which we gladly take part focuses on finding the words to 'say it': to express the vertigo of the turbulence in which our life, our environment, our minds, our sensibilities are cast.[4]

Expressing this turbulence is a way to create harmony where in reality there is chaos. It is in the fluid turbulence of unsafe and uncharted waters that the concept of *passing* moves.

PASSING

1

Obscuring Identity Matrices

My Point of View

With the widening of my visual angle and the re-adjustment to my depth of focus, my viewing lens (through which I perceive our time, all of us, you and myself) has undergone decisive change. It is comparable to the decisive change that occurred more than thirty years ago, when I first became acquainted with Marxist theory and attitudes; a liberating and illuminating experience which altered my thinking, my view, what I felt about and demanded of myself. When I try to realize what is happening and what has happened I find that (to bring it down to the lowest common denominator) there has been an expansion of what for me is "real". Moreover, the nature, the inner structure and the movement of this reality has also changed and continues to change almost daily.

—Christa Wolf
Cassandra[1]

THE MAIN REASON I WROTE THIS BOOK IS THAT THROUGHOUT MY LIFE I often found myself in need of renarrating and redefining myself, to question things that seemed established or rather were taken for granted on account of their narrative and social structure, and to recreate them according to patterns that tended to repeat themselves. Born in Florence, I lived for a long time in the Maremma region in Tuscany—once an unruly border area where bandits were said to roam—and later on decided to move to the United States, where traditionally the experience of being uprooted generates a mythological insecurity, anxiety, and often somewhat artificial identities. These "migrations" forced me to undergo a constant process of deconstruction and reconstruction. Every time I was forced to confront barriers, conscious and unconscious, internal and external, and to fight with countless contradictions and incongruences regarding my individual and social status. Initially, this served to keep me constrained in roles and stereotypes that I felt to be inadequate and that smothered many aspects of myself. But it also taught me the importance of interstices, of marginal spaces, of the space between the lines as the place from which personal history can be reexamined, resisted, and rewritten. Yet, only when I finally severed all ties, which became chains—

whether religious, political, linguistic, ethnic, or sexual—did I experience a truly liberating and joyous moment. However, the phases that preceded and followed this moment have been very painful, full of fear, loneliness, emptiness, feelings of insecurity and guilt, deriving from a sense of having betrayed affections, "causes," values, and memories.

The desire to explain that it is possible to overcome this painful condition by regaining on a permanent basis the fluid multidimensionality of our self, that any sense of belonging inevitably generates a sense of anxiety, limitation, and impoverishment, is the motivation behind this book. There are no betrayals. Affections, memories, ties, and the past are no longer the weight that prevent our dreams from soaring into space. Yet, they do not cease to exist: they live in a state of suspended animation. Their existence is no longer tinted by the deep hue of resentment, but by the delicate nuance of what they no longer are.

To explain that there are other worlds and other words to narrate and to narrate oneself, to experience reality, and that it is sufficient to activate them beyond the control of the dominant narrative that seeks to absorb and dissolve them, is the main purpose of this book.

Understanding that the moment of joy is the moment when you understand that the need not to belong and the phases of disidentification are not a necessary step towards the construction of a new identity, but rather belong to a process of "*deterritorialization*" of the self and of others, this is what I call the experience of *passing.*

Nor does this attitude entail a Zelig-like chamaleonic mutability; rather, it is an ontological form of desire that allows one to communicate, narrate, and experience stories of shifting individuality without remaining faithful to origins and without turning into a "cyborg," though the "cold" provocation of the cyborg is part of a fundamental and extremely sophisticated narrative and political strategy.

Passing, which has in irony its fundamental structural element, means playing with all normative and regulatory notions, beyond all constrictions. It means questioning the rules while the game is still on. It is a process that arises from human action: it can turn us into cyborgs, blurring the boundaries between people and machines, or simply insert our capability of acting and narrating within a mobile grid whose fundamental structure results from a constant crossing of the boundaries of what is defined and definable.

Having once believed, with Hannah Arendt, that politics was the privileged sphere where the existence of all human beings who aspire to liberty should express themselves and having followed this belief without regrets, I remain convinced that the material aspects of our social condition are the fundamental element in the redefinition and renarration of individual stories. At the same time, the belief that the feminist movement and practice represented the beginning of a radical transformation of Western culture, which has been questioned in its most fixed and fossilized millenarian foundations, has influenced and continues to influence in a fundamental way my everyday life, along with the ways I redescribe and narrate my self. All this, therefore, has affected the various identity phases I have undergone and especially the desires and the dreams that have characterized them, as well as the changes and the boundaries of the concept of identity itself.

The fact that these considerations are offered in a period of "transition" like the one we are experiencing is the necessary premise, as Gramsci taught us, for any cultural, political, or social transformation of a more general nature and makes their formulation more problematic, raising questions that we have been trying to answer for some time. The *transitional* condition acquires an unusual relevance when the characteristic mobility of its process is no longer simply an instrument for achieving its goals, but rather becomes an inextricable part of our everyday experience. Within this perspective, many concepts alter their nature, become lighter or even disappear for good. *Identity* is certainly one of these concepts, and understanding its transformation is essential for comprehending if not for directing the changes we are experiencing.

For this reason, I would like to begin narrating myself using categories that are still "heavy," and then gradually proceed to lighten them, to dilute their boundaries, through a process of *disidentification,* that is, of *passing.* Not for the purpose of denying the validity of the reasons behind those categories or the phases they must necessarily undergo in order to become light, but simply because I do not wish those categories to become a prison, separating me from my dreams and from those of other human beings. There are a number of factors, connected to my being a white, heterosexual, Western woman, profoundly influenced by the feminist movement, that certainly trace the boundaries of the area I move in and that continue to have a decisive influence on me. But every time, this influence is explicated in different ways and with different priorities. Also, the fact that I chose to live in a country different from my *original* one imparted to these factors a necessary aura of *foreignness* that was already familiar to me on account of my being a woman.

Certainly, my *point of view* expresses only some of the articulations of subalternity and the positions in which I may situate myself from time to time. The fact that I am a white intellectual, living in relatively privileged economic conditions in a Western country, for example, has allowed me to avoid countless forms of colonization, both in their concrete, material aspects and the associated theoretical perspective. Similarly, as a heterosexual woman, I have been excluded from the exclusively male dominant narrative and social practice, but I have not had to face the problem of lacking a space within the contract of binary sexuality that we all automatically subscribe to, by which we are described, and from which homosexuality or, worse, transgenderism, are erased or removed as radical and subversive elements.

This does not mean that my theoretical elaboration has not been influenced by other *points of view,* belonging to other subjects or other cultures. On the contrary, these are for me essential elements within any process of *disidentification.* The notion that only the person directly experiencing a given event or condition is entitled to speak about it or to subsume it into her or his theoretical and practical "*corpus*" seems to me rather absurd. There often seems to be a tendency to subject experience to rigid copyright rules, rather than trying to move beyond pathological oppositions that describe and circumscribe it. It is my belief, instead, that there is a discrepancy or rather, a double bind between what one is and the position she or he occupies. Certainly, the need of the political and narrative subject to achieve self-legitimation as well as social and discursive spaces is important, but it must not lead to a compartmentalization of the cultural space, with each small yard occupied by a specific variety of subaltern subjects separated from all others. In my view, this is still part of the daily ethics of resentment. This seems to me the ethics behind the Million Man March organized in October 1995 by Louis Farrakhan, who turned the condition of being black into a question of whether or not one was a male with a given color, rather than using it as a category that embraces all the subjects that have experienced or are experiencing marginalized conditions outside the dominant narrative and culture, whether they be Asian, Indian, Jewish, or female. In fact, the attitude of the Nation of Islam is alien to my perspective insofar as it is not by self-proclamation that a *point of view* acquires the power of responding to the needs of the minority it represents, but through its power to articulate and mobilize that minority. Elements that originate in other cultures and subjects are therefore privileged points of observation and narration. They become ways of experiencing differences without being coopted into the demagogic and centralizing "transformism" of a single dominant interpretation, which relativizes any knowledge or cultural fact outside its sphere, disempowering it and making it arbitrary. These elements, instead, can serve to dismantle the rigid borders that limit desire, allowing people *to communicate and feel through multiple eyes and multiple bodies.* They allow them to narrate stories in different languages and from different perspectives, in a constant play of references to *simulacra* which, having lost all their original reference and all possibilities of establishing social and narrative hierarchies, can no longer aspire to "purity," "authenticity," "objectivity," or "transparency."

It is important, in my opinion, to specify that my interest is directed more towards *subcultural* forms rather than *countercultural* ones, because the latter, as Dick Hebdige notes in the wake of Roland Barthes, are characterized "by the explicitly political and ideological forms of its opposition to the dominant culture . . . by its elaboration of 'alternative' institutions. . . . Whereas, opposition in subculture is, as we have seen, displaced into symbolic forms of resistance, the revolt of the middle-class youth, tends to be more articulate, more confident, more directly expressed and is, therefore, as far as we are concerned, more easily 'read.' "[1] Hebdige is clearly focusing on the obscurity of subcultural forms, on their contradictions, on the fact that they represent an *underworld,* and, unlike countercultures, they can avoid being comprehended and mastered by the dominant culture. It is in this perspective that the Gramscian distinction between *domination* and *hegemony* becomes relevant to the present situation. Hegemony is characterized by "dynamic equilibrium," which includes power relations that are both favorable and unfavorable to a given tendency. Writes Hebdige: "[t]he consensus can be fractured, challenged, overruled, and resistance to the groups in dominance cannot always be lightly dismissed or automatically incorporated."[2] According to Hebdige, therefore, the forms of hegemony represented by these subcultures are never directly exhibited, but always couched in an oblique style. "The objections are lodged, the contradictions displayed . . . at the profoundly superficial level of appearances: that is, at the level of signs."[3]

The *style* of subcultures resists and evades the normalization process. This is what Hebdige finds interesting. And it is this aspect, the strategy of resistance and evasion that these cultures enact in regards to the dominant one that I wish to concentrate on.

Some of the theories that directly or indirectly address the problem of the *crisis of identity* will be analyzed in this brief study. I will begin my survey by discussing some critics of the feminist area, the one that has had the greatest influence on me, and then I will venture into to the area of black culture, subsequently into what has been somewhat superficially and generically defined as *postcolonial* English speaking culture, and, finally, I will examine some aspects of native American culture. This will be the background of passing, to which the entire second part of the book will be dedicated. On the one hand, passing can be defined as an instrument for the dissolution of constructed identities because it serves to question that structure. On the other hand, it eliminates separations between isolated groups. Passing is an answer to the problem of identity within postmodern society, a politics of positioning, an experience that questions the solidity that characterizes all subjects, even those that are in a state of crisis. The *transitional* element becomes essential insofar as it is no longer a means toward a given end, but an end in itself.

Passing is a way of conceptualizing psychopolitical dynamics that structure the experience of each one of us; it consists in a state of constant crossing of borders, allowing the expression of fluidity and of the plurality of desire. It is the rediscovery of the self, undermining at the very roots the authenticity of the self. It is not a passing *for someone else,* but an entrance into a foreign and unknown area of the self that had always been taken for granted. It is something that never occurs on a conscious level, notwithstanding the desire to control it and to practice it "correctly." It moves in the futuristic perspective of Donna Haraway, who elaborates through the cyborgs the radical possibility of questioning the very idea of nature, exasperating the narrative of survival. It is a moment of liberation from the Origin and from the shackles of stereotypes and rigid models enmeshed in all sorts of binarisms. But it is also a process that does not require any final end, other than the continuous transition of desire that is an essential part of its being and of its becoming: here and now passing redesigns processes of stratification, the boundaries of categories and the symbolic universe, which we continuously elaborate and reelaborate in a perspective where technology plays a fundamental role in redefining our daily life and the capacity to narrate it. The future is already here and now. As a woman, the first step I wish to take in this process is to retrace the *feminist trail* that has marked the phases of this voyage.

The Feminist Trail

For a moment then I felt a sort of tormented happiness in my entire body, a horrible ill happiness in which my legs seem to give out beneath me, as always when the depth of my identity was touched.

—Clarice Lispector
Passion according to G. H.[1]

THE STARTING POINT OF MY JOURNEY INSIDE THE FEMINIST WORLD IS THE "*theory of sexual difference.*" This phase of women's cultural production originated theoretically and politically with Carla Lonzi and Luce Irigaray, in different periods and according to diverse modalities. It has been developed, in Italy, by the "Diotima" group of women philosophers in Verona. The principle of *sexual difference* as seen by Carla Lonzi is connected to the different roles of man and woman prescribed by the traditional stereotypes of society. This principle pertains to the female gender and distinguishes it from the male gender. Women cannot be defined in relation to men insofar as they are "others," though historically men have always defined women in relation to themselves. Lonzi writes: "Man has always spoken in name of the human race, but half of the world's population now accuses him of having sublimated a mutilation. Man's strength lies in his identification with culture, ours in its rejection. After this conscious act, man will be distinct from woman and will have to listen to her in all that concerns her."[2]

This otherness leads Lonzi to see in the principle of *equality,* central to feminist theory and practice from the beginning of the twentieth century up to the 1960s, an ideological tool of female oppression. For Lonzi, the principle of equality does not question male power; indeed, it legitimates it, legitimating woman's subaltern role by assimilating her to the model elaborated by men and purported to be objective. Difference is an existential principle of concrete behavior; it involves the individual experience and everyday life of women.

Luce Irigaray, too, argues that endorsing the notion of equality means adopting a term of comparison that has the authority of the male model as its privileged reference point, thus legitimating the power of its neutrality and naturalness. The male gender, by presenting itself as "neuter," reifies its partiality and imposes itself as a universally valid model. This cultural configuration, which totalizes the neuter-male, expropriates the genderized subjectivity of women. Women's difference lies in their peculiar relation to language, related to the existence of the body, to the origin of life and to the capability of generating different sexes. It is crucial to establish a principle of difference as a qualifying aspect of the female presence. It is necessary to develop a genderized theory that will reaffirm the importance of gender for each sex. From this perspective, relationships among women are essential, for they allow one to overcome the isolation imposed by society, which traditionally secludes women in the domestic sphere or makes them enter the social sphere only by complying with male models.

The notion of female mediation, essential both to Lonzi and to Irigaray, is the core of the theory of the Diotima group. The Diotima group sees in the theorization of this mediation a basis for the articulation of a political praxis for "saying" oneself and representing oneself in the social sphere. In our society, the existence of a woman is acknowledged only when men "say" her: ". . . through a discourse that *says* her and at the same time denies her because the fact she is not a man *says* her as lacking, as other, as negative. Thus, women undergo the experience of being *said* and at the same time of being denied. Their ontological consistence, their being-there, is divided between answering to the discourse that *says* them and their staying by themselves, without words."[3]

This poses the problem of how "being a woman [can] signify itself" in a symbolic order that defines her in opposition and by similarity to the male sex. From a "thought object" a woman must become a "thinking object," a creative expression of the possibility of alternative forms of mediation capable of constituting a "missing symbolic structure." The separation from the "maternal body," which man struggles to undo by erasing the genealogical process of his origin, expropriates woman's generating power and the power of placing herself at the origin of her word and of her ability to say herself. The transformation must, therefore, occur through a reappropriation of the symbolic order based on that relationship and on the language and cultural tools associated with it. For Luisa Muraro—leader and founder, with others, of the Diotima group—crucial in this regard are the social practices of mediation between women, such as "entrustment," disparity, separate female communities, and homosexuality.

In the field of the "theory of difference," Rosi Braidotti has a special role on account of her originality and theoretical complexity. She attributes to *sexual difference* a nomadic character that certainly lightens it without enfeebling it. Confronted with the choice between a postgender position and the radicalness of a "strategically hyper-sexualized" difference, Braidotti opts for the second solution. She defines it as a "nomadic strategy which favors an extreme affirmation of genderized identity as a way of reversing the attribution of differences."[4] In other words, Braidotti reaffirms sexual difference as a tool essential to the definition of the "feminist woman-subject." This allows one to avoid simplifications that ignore the interweaving of subjective desire and the goal of social transformation, making "alternative forms of feminist political subjectivity" possible: "feminists are the post-woman women." This, according to Braidotti, makes it possible for the "feminist female subject" to act, endowing her with lightness and multidimensionality, turning her into a multiple, open-ended, "interconnected multiple entity."[5] However, Braidotti's effort to "lighten" sexual difference through nomadism is paralleled by a resistance against the efforts to do away with it completely. For Braidotti, there is still an asymmetry between the sexes that justifies its perpetuation. A central *topos* of her theory is the concept of identity, which becomes the site of differences, crucial to the redefinition of female subjectivity.

The essential analysis that has developed through "the theory of difference" runs parallel to another development in feminist theory, equally important in my opinion, made by certain American intellectuals who, while taking gender theory as their starting point, overcome its intrinsic limitations, going beyond the schematic opposition nature/culture, mechanically latent in the sex/gender dualism. The analogy between the opposition gender/culture and the opposition sex/nature, at least in an initial phase, implied a simplification devoid of mobility. Many thinkers (it is important to mention, in this regard, the contribution of Judith Butler) have struggled long and hard with this in an effort to eliminate the traces of determinism that tainted the theory and overcame the dualistic mind/body structure implicit in its oppositions. The common goal of these thinkers is that of liberating feminist theory from a measure of theoretical stasis and from its excessive self-structuring in the social sphere, which, in the present transitional phase, can no longer be independent of the positioning of the feminist subject. In the light of these theoretical developments, the theory of *sexual difference* represents a narrowing space, limiting the freedom and the positioning of the feminist subject—especially in reference to the asymmetry between heterosexual and homosexual theory—since it theorizes the centrality of the man/woman asymmetry to the point of neglecting other possible elements of differentiation. Teresa de Lauretis, for example, sees a danger of essentialism in the theory of difference, since it favors the signifier woman in its difference with man, rather than taking into account the possibility of articulating the differences between women and Woman, that is, the differences between women and within women, due to race, class, age, sexuality, and so on. Another feminist intellectual, Donna Haraway, goes completely beyond the perspective of the theory of difference, redefining the concept of nature, its relation to science and consequently the notion of the body, which is central to the theory of difference but no longer adequate, for Haraway, as a reference model on which a stable identity can be constructed. Haraway positions the subject in fluctuating locations that relativize points-of-view without making them arbitrary. Through "situated knowledges" that transform the connection of world and subject into an interactive space, Haraway positions the embodied subject, a producer of knowledge, by making it aware of the partiality of her contribution, determined by her historical period, her social role, sex, race, age, etc., thus redefining social and community relations.

A short analytical survey of feminist theory, though limited to the thinkers more germane to my approach, is from this perspective a necessary step. I will ransack the repertoire of adverbs of space to express the various positions. Locutions such as *there, elsewhere,* and *somewhere* express, in my view, the most significant positions in the feminist field. At their roots lies the problem of the identification of the subject. The interest of the more recent theoretical production by these intellectuals lies, on the one hand, in their narratives, which skirt the boundaries of the categories within which they operate—whether they be difference, gender, or the idea of nature—and, on the other hand, in the fact that they confront the technology without rejecting it in principle, and even giving it, as in the case of Donna Haraway, an unprecedented centrality. Personally, I hover between one theoretical elaboration and the other, often positioning myself in contradictory and ambiguous ways. While, compared to Braidotti, I would tend to reject the anxiety of identity that still conditions her and emphasize the constant fluidity of *deterritorialization* processes of the self, I am not convinced, on the other hand, that the construction processes inherent in the connection between human being and machine entirely address the necessity for new forms of political and narrative action. In this regard, I feel that the phases through which this process should occur have been insufficiently clarified, or, to use Rosi Braidotti's terminology, that it is unclear how the "consummation of the totemic feast" has occurred. In general, I think it is important to briefly illustrate the central themes of this intellectual landscape through a map which, to some extent, reproduces my own anxieties but also contains a description of what I consider to be the most significant theoretical positions in contemporary feminism.

Feminist theory, according to Braidotti, needs a nonunitary mobility based on three levels; the first level highlights "the difference between man and woman," the second "the differences among women," and the third "the differences within each woman." Leaving aside the first two, the third level, precisely because it belongs to the internal and discontinuous time of female genealogy, seems to me of particular interest, though Braidotti repeatedly affirms that these three levels are more of a "map" than a stratification of categories: they are different faces of a single, articulated phenomenon. In this way, Braidotti engages the complexity of the subjective structure, highlighting the difference between identity processes and consciousness, and attributing it to the former unconscious desire. "The self, meaning an entity endowed with identity, is anchored in this living matter, whose materiality is coded and rendered in language."[6] Technology, as one of the constitutive elements of the self, is seen—differently from Adriana Cavarero, a more orthodox representative of the theory of difference, who considers it a "penetration" into the *bios* of the female body—as a "prospective body," an additional body, which amplifies our functions. This places women in positions characterized by contradiction, but also by great power. Technology multiplies and manipulates bodies, ignoring gender differences and highlighting a crucial difference between Plato's *techné* and present reality, but also exposing his goals. Certainly science can lead us to destruction, but it can also reverse the life/death relationship that has always characterized Western tradition.

While Braidotti does not believe in the inviolability of the body, she has reservations about grafting machines onto humans, the result of the technological hybridization that we are currently witnessing. For example, she criticizes Donna Haraway's cyborg, arguing that it is not enough to claim that sexual identity is "obsolete"; one must also point the way out of a system still based on the asymmetry of sexes. "In other words," writes Braidotti, "I need to pay attention to the level of identity, of unconscious identifications and of desire, and to conjugate those levels with willful political transformations."[7]

While the *cyborg* can be an important tool of political change, it is insufficient, in Braidotti's view, in terms of the definition of identity. Braidotti's *nomadic subject* expresses the need to act both on the level of conscious and unconscious desire. The transformation of psychic reality must not be achieved solely through conscious volition; rather one must travel the "multiple layers of meaning of *woman*"[8] and continue working on them: that is, on women as "feminist female subjects," deconstructing them in order to produce "new kinds of desiring subjects as molecular, nomadic, and multiple."[9] This means living in the paradox of the continuous deconstruction and construction of identity without getting trapped in a new logic of dominion, which would be nothing but an inversion of the servant-master logic.

> This form of consciousness combines features that are usually perceived as opposing, namely the possession of a sense of identity that rests not on fixity but on contingencies. The nomadic consciousness combines coherence with mobility. It aims to rethink the unity of the subject without reference to dualistic beliefs, without dualistic opposition, linking instead body and mind in a new set of intensive and often intransitive transitions.[10]

Braidotti's nomadism is "active" in the sense that it does not accept marginalization and advocates a sort of mass exodus from the "logocentric *polis,*" questioning its capacity to transform its power structure. This radical position is countered, however, by the belief that "being a nomad, living in transition, does not mean that one cannot or is unwilling to create those necessarily stable and reassuring bases for identity that allow one to function in a community."[11]

While I appreciate Braidotti's theorizing of nonpermanent identities, I have difficulty understanding how the "actualization of the nomad image" can be conceived in terms of a reassuring return to institutional borders: "The best way to render the image of the nomad in a concrete matter is by translating it into institutional politics."[12] It is my impression that Braidotti's rejection of an identity characterized by "fluidity without borders," which she replaces with the "non-permanence of borders," is quite remote from Donna Haraway's perspective of "situated knowledges" (tending to the extreme and radical invention of the *cyborg,* which sweeps away the idea of borders itself and that of identity). In my view, Braidotti's position certainly leads to a "lightening" of the theory of difference, but remains inscribed inside the above *polis,* the *polis* we do not trust and do not wish to enter, as Carla Lonzi suggested. The *theres* of place that characterize this theoretical position are therefore the various statements found in the enunciation, which define the *signifier woman* in a material and discursive sense. The "theres" of this nomadism assume "sexual difference as that which offers mobile locations for multiple feminist and female embodied voices"[13] in which, however, the structure of identity maintains an essential role, even though decentralizing and decentralized.

While I agree with Braidotti that sexual asymmetry continues to exist and still carries some weight and, therefore, that, in many situations, it is necessary to continue thinking in terms of sexual difference, I am not so sure that the nomadic process through which the change must take place should have as its goal the creation of stable, albeit nonpermanent, foundations for new identities in order to reconstruct multiple subjects that would be at ease within communal spaces. In my view, it is the concept of community itself that must change, becoming mobile and producing a network of social relations that continuously change, making the process of belonging transitory. Braidotti thinks the question should be addressed in terms of the acknowledgment of the need to respect multiplicity by finding forms of female praxis that would reflect its complexity without being swallowed by it. I believe, instead, that the emphasis should be on the fluidity of the borders, on movement and changes of state—facilitated by our being women—rather than on the identity teleology of the new subjects.

Teresa de Lauretis's central idea is a modified version of the concept of gender, which makes it easier to overcome the dualism implicit in the theory of difference and to articulate the multiplicity of differences. For de Lauretis, such a concept does not belong to the body "nor is it something originally existent in human beings . . . [it is] the product and the process of a number of social technologies, of techno-social or biomedical apparati."[14] These technological constructions shape gender, considered as a "representation and self-representation," and are constituted by cinema, institutional discoveries, different epistemologies and critical and daily praxis. This interpretation of gender opens the way to a heteronomous multiplicity, which privileges its construction as a product of technical and discursive strategies. The notion of technology, used in a Foucaldian sense, must be understood as equivalent to a multiplicity of discourses, positions and meanings, often in conflict with one another, having as its main object the simultaneous deconstruction and the construction of gender. The differences among women cannot be elements of a fixed and stable identity precisely on account of their intimately contradictory nature. By means of a continuous movement in and out of gender, they serve to define the female subject of feminism. The intent of de Lauretis is to overcome the ideological limits and limitations that the notion of "sexual difference" has imposed on feminist critical thought. Because of its essentialism, the theory of "sexual difference" ends up perpetuating patriarchal structures of discourse and praxis since it continues to move within the confines of that theoretical apparatus, using its intellectual instruments, "the master's tools," to adopt Audré Lorde's expression. Going beyond the limits of Foucault's "technology of sex"—which does not distinguish between the needs of male and female subjects or identify the conflict of interests latent in the discourse of sexuality—de Lauretis situates the "gendered female subject" at the same time inside and outside the ideology of gender, based on a "multiple subject" facing the ideological apparatuses and the sociocultural technologies of gender.

For de Lauretis, the critique of the theories of gender is vital because it opens up the possibility "to create new spaces of discourse, to rewrite cultural narratives and to define the terms of another perspective—a view from *elsewhere*."[15] The space where one moves is continuously dislocated and the *elsewhere* is constituted by marginal spaces within hegemonic discourse. It is precisely in these spaces that we must find the possibility of modifying the construction of gender, whose terms involve questions of subjectivity and self-representation. The spaces of women's everyday political praxis and cultural production are characterized by a movement *into* and *out* of ideology, going *to* and *fro* across the boundaries and limits of sexual difference—or rather of sexual differences, as de Lauretis would say—thus constituting the *elsewhere* that genderizes the subject of feminism. For de Lauretis, this movement does not represent an exit from a discursive space and the entrance into the real one. Rather, the movement takes place within the representation of gender: in the interstice between represented spaces and nonrepresented (or rather unseen) spaces, whether found within discourse, within the sex/gender system, or within representation itself. De Lauretis's area of specialization is film studies, and she uses the technical term "space off" to describe the location where this "sexualizing" of gender takes place.

The work of literary deconstruction done by the Italian writer Dacia Maraini on Flaubert's *Madame Bovary* is a brilliant example of "space off." In *Cercando Emma* (Searching for Emma), Maraini analyzes the character of Emma Bovary, an archetypal figure of women's liberation. While moving within the space of a male dominant narrative (Flaubert's), she continuously switches between this space and the marginal spaces of female representation. Maraini reconstructs, detective-like, the relation of the author to his character analyzing the beliefs implicit in the text, the emphasis found in certain descriptions, the modality through which the character is constructed, the dynamics of her actions and reactions, and the concentration or lack thereof on given aspects of Emma's character and social role. Through her deconstruction of the development of Flaubert's "most hated and beloved" character and an analysis of Flaubert's epistolary, Maraini uncovers the writer's profound misogyny, which appears as the result of the repression of a strong female aspect of his personality. In this way, Maraini uncovers de Lauretis's *elsewhere* as a place for reading and interpreting, that is, as a place where a female reading of the text can be carried out, constructing a process of genderization of a narrative and a feminist praxis. Maraini moves, therefore, between two spaces: the dominant narrative of the author and the space outside the narrative, in a constant tension between *to* and *fro, inside* and *outside,* which ontologically describes the theoretical and practical condition of feminism.

De Lauretis explains in theoretical terms what this continuous movement means: "to live a contradiction which I have suggested is the condition of feminism here and now: the tension of a twofold pull in contrary directions—the critical negativity of its theory and the affirmative positivity of its politics—is both, the historical condition of feminism and its theoretical possibility. The subject of feminism is engendered right here."[16]

The multiplicity of the feminist subject is, therefore, determined by the *elsewhere* that is continuously dislocated between the lines, between marginal spaces and the central and hegemonic spaces of narration, through diverse fields and knowledges. This continuous movement, riddled with contradictions, provides an image of the representation of feminism that is never consistent and monolithic. The emphasis on the contradictions of the feminist subject is the greatest merit of this thinker, who presents the feminist diaspora as an unavoidable reality, locating the limitations of the concept of gender precisely in the heterosexual contract on which it is based.

Donna Haraway's position is different, being based on a significant change of perspective. The theme of gender is set aside, along with that of difference, and the author concentrates on the idea of nature. For Haraway, gender depends on the body's location, but the body must not be reified, but considered as a semiotic, material prosthesis, which produces meaning. Donna Haraway's famous theoretical construction, the "cyber organism," is the result of a reflection on the fact that nature is not a given, but is always constructed. The cyborg "is a cybernetic organism, a hybrid of machine and organism, a creature of social reality as well as a creature of fiction."[17] It belongs to a postgender world from which the category of wholeness is banished. It represents the overcoming of all dualisms and turns irony and partiality into essential tools. Cyborgs can position themselves anywhere. But what makes them unsettling and dangerous is the fact that when they choose their position, they coldly and decidedly aim for the heart of the designated target. They break the formal boundaries of human identity, situating themselves at the intersection of human, machine, and animal. They represent a sort of profane promiscuity that goes beyond a rigid concept of identity, shattering it. They translate the world into codifications that privilege disassembling and reassembling processes rather than trying to pursue the project of a common language. This mobility unveils the impossibility of an "innocent" identity and demonstrates the importance of situated critical knowledges, capable of opening networks of connections and altering the political and epistemological universe.

Totalization and relativism, promising "a view from everywhere and nowhere," are banned from this theoretical position in favor of an objectivity that "privileges contestation, deconstruction, passionate construction, webbed connections and hope for transformation of systems of knowledge and ways of seeing."[18] The mobile location of knowledges, for Haraway, is inversely proportional to the idea of identity constructions, inherent in the vision of the self. The "visual" knowledge system, which has guided the construction of the self in the past, is now undergoing an irreversible crisis. Feminist thought has the charge of revisualizing inverted worlds as a challenge to the patriarchal perspective. Haraway envisions nonisomorphic subjects, whose stories are not visible and cannot be absorbed by the "cyclopic eye of Western culture," which belongs to the unitary identity of its subject. A contradictory and divided self permits diverse and heterogeneous positionings. For Haraway, "*splitting* in this context should be about heterogeneous multiplicities that are simultaneously necessary and incapable of being squashed into isomorphic slots or cumulative lists."[19] A partially knowing self, whose morphological syntax is never complete but always fluid, continuously reconstructs itself and, therefore, is capable of connecting with the vision of the other without becoming the other. Objectivity must not be sought in the subjective position of identity, but in its partial connection. Science is not produced through mutable identifications adopted by the subject, but only through the critical positioning of a divided and multidimensional self.

The knowing self—for Haraway—is partial in all its manifestations, never finished, never whole, never simply there as original; it is always constructed and imperfectly assembled and, therefore, capable of connecting with the other, capable of seeing together with the other without claiming to be the other. This is the promise of objectivity: the person who wishes to approach science must look for the subject's position, not for the identity. The search for a "full" and total position is the search for the fetishized perfect subject of oppositional history, sometimes appearing in feminist theory as the essentialized Woman of the Third World. As Haraway notes, this search for a subjective totality enacted by a whole and stable subject is the characteristic obsession of the processes of self-mirroring of the subject, which characterizes the Western patriarchal philosophical and scientific tradition. Only eyes and bodies, which are "incarnated," that is "situated," constantly changing their position and connections, make knowing possible.

Within this strategy of gnosis, *cyborg* narrative is founded on the power to resist and survive. Its tools are often retold stories, versions that subvert and displace the hierarchical dualisms of naturalized identities. In retelling the stories of the origin, cyborg authors subvert the central myths of the origin of Western culture. "Feminist *cyborg* stories," writes Haraway, "have the task of re-coding communication and intelligence to subvert command and control."[20] Their narrative goes against all forms of perfect communication, against the transparency of the signifier. "Stripped of identity the bastard race teaches the power of the margins."[21]

The model of scientific knowledge criticized by Haraway is the one that purports to be an objective vision from "nowhere," which implies the possibility of positioning oneself "everywhere," typical of the desire for transcendental omnipotence of Western epistemology, which always yearned to turn man into an indifferent god. Against this model, Haraway advocates knowledges *from somewhere,* so that, having peeled the "layers from the onion," a range of possibilities is left based not on relativism, but on the relativity of points of view, producing objective, but limited, knowledges. The central aspect of this cognitive process is a conception of nature not as a passive element to dominate but as an active element that we must reexamine and with which we must recreate a mutual relationship, according to different aspects and points of view. Within this model, the relationship with the body and with the identities through which the body moves is seen in an entirely different light. The body is no longer a permanently defined entity but one that is defined variously according to the position and the social interactions of the new subject. This subject is the cyborg, in which the relationship with the flesh has gone beyond physiological barriers, positioning itself in the area of the posthuman. Its image and concrete positioning *somewhere* signify its overcoming of dualisms (mind/body, organism/machine, and nature/culture, to cite only a few), which belong to the unitary logic typical of total and monodimensional identities.

In each of these three thinkers, I detect an attention to the importance of marginality, multiplicity, desire and mobility, even though with different and sometimes opposite characteristics, as in the case of Braidotti and Haraway. The effort to find spaces for the female voice—whether arising from the multiplicity of the nomadic feminist female subject, or the contradictory interplay of spaces and knowledges continuously moving between the hegemonic and marginal spaces of everyday life and discourse, or expressed in the unstable positioning of the cyborgs—remains central to their theories. In all three, in different ways, I see the search for the possibility of a political praxis and narrative that would acknowledge the articulations of the female voice as subversive, as dislocating or undermining the dominant voice, as constituting a destabilizing space in Western cultural, technological, and biological tradition.

I accept Braidotti's invitation not to ignore, indeed to narrate, the necessary transformation phases that we must undergo, if we wish to escape from the patriarchal logic of identity and respond to the need for constant mobility expressed by de Lauretis and for the unstable location of Haraway's cyborg. It is my opinion that a period of itinerating and situated temporality must be introduced for the purpose of not turning the past either into an object of resentment and an unbearable burden or into useless and easily discarded baggage. Here the cyborg inevitably plays a role. It is precisely this aspect that mitigates the danger of its being the illegitimate child of "militarism patriarchal, capitalism, and state socialism" because it convinces it of the necessity of being unfaithful to its origins. By emphasizing the time-lag in the emergence of a female subject in the history of modernity, my goal is not to provide an origin to a still to be written history but simply to stress a peculiarity that pertains also to other subjects and still exposes them to the danger of being colonized within the spaces of the dominant culture and narrative. My goal is to explain how this time lag, in different ways, has created the experience of *not being there,* that is, of not being on the stage of history when it was narrated.

If, with Fanon, we consider the displacement of subaltern subjects, we see that the problem cannot be solved through a "spacialization" of the time of modernity à la Foucault, since this would be a Eurocentric way of approaching the problem. As Homi Bhabha reminds us, this universalizing effort, based on an empty and homogeneous time applied to everybody, deprives cultural communities of their differences, and also of those marginal spaces where they can narrate themselves and differentiate themselves from the dominant narrative. Therefore the concept of *time lag* elaborated by Bhabha represents a form of "belatedness," which, interrupting the linear idea of progress, creates a coupure and separation in the dominant narrative. It shows the existence of subjects who in the past did not take part in the process of history of modernity. Today their stories represent an eccentric position in living and telling stories; "Time-lag keeps alive the making of the past"[22] writes Bhabha, not in the sense of a return to the past, of an emphasis on the origin, or a retro-version of it to be introduced again later into the linearity of the idea of progress. Instead, it is the concept of "*projective past*" that acts on the present, reviving its dead symbols in order to remind us that those who have experienced the nightmare of absence and oppression have survived: "Without the postcolonial time-lag the discourse of modernity cannot, I believe, be written; with the *projective past* it can be inscribed as a historical narrative of alterity that explores forms of social antagonism and contradiction that are not yet properly represented, political identities in the process of being formed, cultural enunciations in the act of hybridity, in the process of translating and transvaluing cultural differences."[23]

This process challenges the identity of all of us and points out the lack of authenticity and solidity of the self. The female characters of Toni Morrison, for example, are always pursued by their past. Yet, this past does not break into the present with the weight of resentment or to bear witness to the hermeneutics of progress. Her characters represent the existence of other discursive forms and locations. They bear witness to the break in the idea of a linear progress typical of Western modernity and the enduring existence of discursive and political models in which the marginality of certain subjects is at the same time a precondition and a destabilizing presence for the existence of the dominant subjects. Ella, one of Toni Morrison's characters, expresses this concept very well when she says:

> The future was sunset; the past something to leave behind. And if it didn't stay behind you might have to stomp it out. The life of a slave; a free life—everyday was an experiment, a rehearsal. Nothing could have value in a world when even when you were a solution you were a problem [. . . .] As long as the ghost showed out from its ghostly place – making things shake, crying, and destroying things . . . Ella respected it. But if it took flesh and came in her world, well, the shoe was on the other foot. She didn't mind a little communication between the two worlds, but this was an invasion.[24]

Thus the past, like the ghost in Morrison's story, is not necessarily something that refers to an origin or limits the range of affiliations, but something that can represent, through the idea of *time-lag,* a mobile space in time that has the specific purpose of reminding us of how the presence of certain subjects, including the female one, is marked by an absence that does not seek to turn itself into an ethics of resentment on which a new history must be based. On the contrary, it becomes a privileged tactical weapon through which one can escape the clutches of the idea of unending progress that flattens our peculiarities, as well as the equally sharp claws of a narrative based on our exclusion. The *rage* and *outlandishness* produced by a history of oppression can be transformed into a capacity for irony, which, altering the weight of the myths of origin, allows us to relive and retell our stories, saving us from blind mechanisms that would lock us inside the narrow cages of stereotypes. This is how the time-lag, as an instrument of communication internal and external to us, provides the possibility and the reason for dislocating and subverting dominant social narratives and practices, becoming a localizing element of our voice and an important step toward possible disidentification processes. It allows us to deal with a past that, because it has excluded us, forces us to confront the *rage* and violence that this exclusion has produced. It also presents us with the option of lightness and movement, making it easier to escape the limitations of what is defined and to create new theoretical structures and categories connected to different ways of living and desiring. This is particularly evident in those subaltern ethnic cultures that are forced to confront the genealogy of their origins and the tradition through which they reconnect their principles of belonging.

Killing Rage

> They approach me in a half-hesitant sort of way, eye me curiously or compassionately, and then, instead of saying directly, How does it feel to be a problem? they say, I know an excellent colored man in my town . . . Do not these Southern outrages make your blood boil? At these I smile, or am interested, or reduce the boiling to a simmer, as the occasion may require. To the real question: "How does it feel to be a problem?" I answer seldom a word.
>
> —W. E. B. Du Bois, *The Souls of Black Folk*[1]

THE ENDLESS DEBATE ON MULTICULTURALISM IN THE UNITED STATES draws attention to those ethnic and racial identities that seek to emerge without being sucked into the whirlpool of the dominant white Anglo-Saxon culture. The *melting pot* has failed to produce even a decent salad. The attempt to combine various traditions in a single American way of life has failed. It has been replaced by the idea of *multiculturalism,* which aspires to preserve the various cultural and linguistic affiliations without altering the values and the canon that underlie the "American Dream" as elaborated by the dominant culture. Nowadays, the United States must face the consequences of these mistakes and of the failure of its strategy. Two widely divergent paths have been chosen. The white elite, in demographic decline, has opted for an aggressive right-wing policy, highly structured and *territorialized.* The enormous ethnic and racial mosaic, which in a few years will become the majority of the population, expresses its disorientation in confused and contradictory ways. Sometimes it chooses or accepts ruthless integration, which deprives individuals of their past, often with disastrous personal and social consequences. At other times, it withdraws its visibility and thus resists integration into the dominant culture. Sometimes its reactions erupt in violence that express these people's marginalization and, by the same token, their refusal to be squeezed into a single cultural model. But all these reactions lead to fractures, racial divisions, misconceptions, and demands that are still basically the result of a racist mentality. Countless words have been spent on this subject, but Malcolm X remains one of the few who has lucidly analyzed, for the black community, the origins and character of racism in America, a racism that produces on the one hand politicians such as Buchanan and, at the other extreme, ambiguous, fanatic figures like Farrakhan.

Unlike Martin Luther King, Malcolm X was the prophet of black *rage* as an element of subversion of white supremacy. But, as Cornel West has noted, Malcolm X's "rage," articulated in an unprecedented fashion during the sixties, was a symbol of his love for the black race, "was a concrete connection with a degraded and devalued people in need of a psychic conversion."[2] Malcolm X's goal was to decolonize the minds of American blacks, freeing them from white cultural standards and restoring the dignity they had lost through the racist values incorporated into their everyday behavior. According to bell hooks, however, the effort to merge rage and love does not define that rage as a "passion for justice, that may not emerge from the context of that great love. West attempts to explain *that* rage away, to temper it. Overall contemporary reassessments of Malcolm X's political career tend to deflect away from the *killing rage*."[3] On the contrary, for bell hooks it is important not to eliminate the rage from the antiracist struggle, not to repress it or justify it, because this would mean playing to the white audience's expectations. In fact, the rage is a necessary step in a liberating process that needs to be translated into a political form. White supremacy, as an aggregation of cultural and social values that becomes interiorized in the everyday life of whites and blacks alike, always tends to provide a pathological interpretation of black rage rather than identify the structure within which the rage expresses itself. Malcolm X's rage was not directed only against whites but also against those blacks who subscribed to the interpretative categories imposed by white domination. According to bell hooks, it is essential to affirm its importance as a radical element of antiracist struggle, also within the black community, which believes it is exempt from it.

Even if Malcolm X's insistence on autonomy and separatism was ultimately the product of a deep-seated fear of hybridity, his "psychic conversion" had the legitimate purpose of producing a sense of self-esteem that would make the black community capable of self-government. This transformation was centered on the idea that the space where the black community could cultivate love, interest, care, and solidarity for itself could only be created by the rage that slavery, segregation, and, finally, the subaltern position within American society, had produced. But, according to Cornel West, it is precisely at this point that Malcolm X's project falters insofar as it fails to channel this positive energy into a political action that would place black cultural hegemony within a cultural and political project beyond the simple reversion of the status quo. Malcolm X's joining of the Nation of Islam did little to help his cause. The adoption of Islamic theology was a hindrance to political goals of a progressive nature. This was evident when, in October 1995, Louis Farrakhan—present leader of the Nation of Islam and self-proclaimed direct and legitimate heir of Malcolm X, promoted his "Million Man March," excluding women and sending threatening messages to other minorities. His anti-Semitic and anti-Asian statements are well-known and so is the male chauvinism of his internal organization, structured along hierarchical military lines. His speech, delivered in Washington in front of six-hundred-thousand blacks, was a mixture of apocalyptic religious terminology and elements of black popular music, from the "call" of God in favor of the redemption of blacks to the rap music techniques used by his bodyguards, who during the speech constantly incited the audience, rhythmically chanting at regular intervals the words "you're all right" and "go ahead." Thus, the call for a mass mobilization against white America was based on the assertion of a strong, authentic, winning identity to be used against the enemy.

Malcolm X's message, therefore, may be used by the nationalist advocates of black supremacy even though his idea of psychic conversion had as its primary goal the rejection of captivity as a product of the ideology and praxis of white supremacy. The civil rights movement was not militant enough for him—as Cornel West has pointed out. On the other hand, what remains unclear is the connection between black rage and concepts such as cultural hybridity, black supremacy, authoritarianism, the boundaries of sexuality, and other controversial issues. It is important to stress that the black community must reject binarism and authoritarianism. In other words, the rage should be aimed against racism, sexism, homophobia, and economic injustice, which prevent common people from living with dignity. It is for this purpose that Cornel West and Michael Lerner (founder and editor of the liberal Jewish journal *Tikkun*) have decided to publish *Jews and Blacks: Let the Healing Begin,* where the necessity of healing the wounds inflicted by racial tensions in contemporary America is the starting point of a political reflection that seeks to go beyond the concepts of ethnic, religious, or sexual identity. The rage should not lead to actions based on resentment; rather, it should be part of a flexibility that would allow people to overcome the idea of supremacy and dogmatism. The risk, according to West, is falling victim to extremely dangerous forms of nihilism that are also expression of a rage, a pathological and self-destructive rage, chiefly directed against the black community itself and especially against women, its most vulnerable subjects. Writes West:

> Sadly, the combination of the market way of life, poverty-ridden conditions, black existential angst and the lessening fear of white authorities has directed most of the anger, rage and despair toward fellow black citizens, especially toward black women, who are the most vulnerable in our society and in black communities. Only recently has this nihilistic threat—and its ugly inhuman outlook and actions—surfaced in the larger American society. And its appearance surely reveals one of the many instances of cultural decay in a declining Empire.[4]

These self-destructive tendencies found inside the black community must be countered; it is against this threat and towards a policy of conversion that the effort of black intellectuals and politicians must be directed. Following Malcolm X's project, West suggests that one focus on concepts such as love and nurturing, not as the basis for sentimentalism or tribal connections but as instruments for generating a new capability for action springing from self-esteem and self-affirmation. And this should be done without underestimating the pervasive influence of the economic structure and the resiliency of nihilistic tendencies.

In fact, the problem of violent and self-destructive tendencies within the black community is central in black culture. Spike Lee's *Clockers* dramatically evidences this issue. The two main characters, a black teenage pusher called Strike and the elderly white cop called Rocco, are individuals with complex and multifaceted personalities. Yet they inhabit a universe structured by dualisms that limit the scope of their self-expression, making it almost impossible for them to relate to one another outside the boundaries of established roles and communicative stereotypes. And for all that, they somehow manage to establish a meaningful connection. Environmental degradation, violence, gangs of black teenage pushers—who are both victims and perpetrators of daily violence—the constant police searches, and a murder that young Strike is commissioned: this is the context in which the two characters have to interact. The novelty of the movie lies in the fact that both figures strive to overcome the racist ideologies pitting one against the other. Both characters rebel against the destructive and self-destructive violence that surrounds them. The mixture of cynicism and humanity in the cop and of naiveté and complete amorality in the pusher certainly reveal desperation and rage, and white supremacy and the current segregation of blacks. Yet, in the movie amidst the sadness inspired by the degraded condition of the black community, we also find hope, a desire to overcome the dualisms that lie at the root of racism.

Against all expressions of rigidity and dogmatism is bell hooks, who, in an article significantly titled "Black Identity: Liberating Subjectivity," affirms her belief that there is no unitary representation of *blackness* on which a given subjectivity can be constructed. West and bell hooks share the view that there is no monolithic black community and no normative identity. They question the concept of black authenticity as the essence of a subjectivity that is actually much more complex and cannot be reduced to a single perspective. The difference between the two is that for West the theorization of identity must be done in relation to *white supremacy,* while for bell hooks this process must be carried out from multiple locations, not only in terms of race, but in terms of class, sexual practices, etc.; that is, all those locations that are part of the construction of the self. For bell hooks there is unquestionably an identity crisis in *blackness,* and an essentialist and reactionary line of thinking, still enmeshed in dominant categories and binarisms; she cannot imagine its representation in unitary and stable terms. It is this crisis and this mutable situation that we must reckon with. Writes bell hooks:

> While it certainly is important for black folks to foreground discussions of white supremacy, it is equally important for us to affirm that liberation takes place only in a context where we are able to imagine subjectivities that are diverse, constantly changing, and always operating in states of cultural contingency. To embrace and accept fluid black subjectivities, African-American attachment to a notion of the unitary self must be broken. African Americans must embrace the progressive political understanding of diasporic black identity [. . .] . Psychoanalytically, it is clear that the unitary self is sustained only by acts of coercive control and repression. Collectively African Americans fear the loss of a unitary representation of blackness because they feel we will lose a basis for organized resistance [. . .] . Fluidity means that our black identities are constantly changing as we respond to circumstances in our families and communities of origin, and as we interact with a larger world. Only by privileging the reality of that changing black identity will we be able to engage a prophetic discourse about subjectivity that will be liberating and transformative.[5]

The belief that the emergence of cultural hybridities and the possibility of crossing cultural and ethnic boundaries are necessary to overcome racism is central for both intellectuals. Though belonging to the most radical wing of black leadership, they see the affirmation of strong identities, celebrated by nationalist and fundamentalist currents, as self-destructive weapons that do nothing but confirm white supremacy.

Bell hooks also discusses the fact that capitalist patriarchy hinders identity formation in black women, creating a profound sense of isolation but also an uncommon lightness. We find it represented, for example, in the main character of Tony Morrison's novel *Sula:* "The first experience taught her there was no other that you could count on; the second that there was no *self* to count on either. She had no center, no speck around which to grow. [. . .] She was completely free of ambition, with no affection for money, property or things, no greed, no desire to command attention or compliments—no ego. For that reason she felt no compulsion to verify herself—be consistent with herself."[6]

Whether we call it *solidarity politics* like bell hooks, or *conversion politics* like Cornel West, what we are dealing with is a celebration of protean, fluid dispositions that seek to overcome dualistic and disjunctive logic. Cornel West uses the metaphor of jazz, referring especially to the practice of improvisation and jam sessions, in order to express the need for agile forms of cultural hybridity, quickly adapting to everyday life and signifying the coagulation of individual energies into larger groups, within which black rage may be transformed. From an element of the struggle against white supremacy, it acquires a broader sense, while critically acknowledging the forms of misogyny, homophobia, and authoritarianism intrinsic in the present society:

> To be a jazz freedom fighter is to attempt to galvanize and energize world-weary people into forms of organization with accountable leadership that promote critical exchange and broad reflection [. . .] . Black people's rage should not overlook homophobia, yet also should acknowledge that heterosexuality *per se* can be associated with so-called straight anti-homophobes—just as the struggle against black poverty can be supported by progressive elements of any race, gender or sexual orientation.[7]

Bell hooks addresses the same issue when she proposes the creation of *beloved communities,* where all the subjects belonging to subaltern cultures or ethnic groups, would ally themselves, overcoming their differences, affiliations, and exclusive ties. In such communities original traditions would mingle to the point where it becomes impossible to separate them. This represents a critique of the notion of multiculturalism as an ensemble of separate cultures and identities bent on marking and defending its exclusive territory, oblivious to the fact that *white supremacy* is what dictates its values and ideals. As bell hooks notes:

> A progressive *politics of solidarity* that embraces both a broad-based identity politics which acknowledges specific cultural and ethnic legacies, histories, etc., as it simultaneously promotes recognition of overlapping cultural traditions and values as well as an inclusive understanding of what is gained when people of color unite to resist white supremacy is the only way to ensure that multicultural democracy will become a reality.[8]

Taking the original elaboration of Malcolm X as their starting point, both Cornel West and, more radically, bell hooks stress the importance of black rage without theorizing, however, a separatism based on resentment or inverted racism. The main goal of these two intellectuals is not the construction of monolithic organizations based on strong identity processes due to the color of the skin, past slavery, or the need to secure privileged power positions. On the contrary, for both of them black rage is the basis for constructive change and a weapon against indifference. "I care" was a popular slogan of American students during the sixties. It is precisely to this combination of indignation and the desire to participate in a general transformation that black rage must be related. In his movie *Malcolm X,* Spike Lee makes the leader's detachment from the Nation of Islam a central episode. At one point in the movie, Malcolm X realizes that the ideals he was fighting for have been abandoned by his most trusted comrades, among them Elijah Muhammad, the leader of the Nation of Islam at the time. In the movie, this *betrayal* becomes the central drama of his existence but also the event that opens new horizons, the turning point in his political strategy. From that moment, Malcolm X conceives the idea of involving in the process of transformation of American society all minorities and all those, including whites, who are willing to fight against white supremacy. Thus, from a betrayal arises the will to struggle against indifference, no longer in terms of fundamentalist violence aimed at the simple reversal of the situation and the establishment of the counterculture as the dominant culture, but through the alliance of different subaltern subjects struggling together against all forms of racism and separatism. It is at this point that Malcolm X reconsiders his attitude toward Martin Luther King, the pacifist movement, and the notion of the indiscriminate use of violence as a strategy for change.

In fact, it is this latter aspect that I would like to focus on. While I certainly do not conceive of violence as an indiscriminately suitable instrument of change, I do see it as a presence in our daily lives that cannot be ignored without losing a considerable part of our humanity. Therefore, some violence should be recovered in our daily practices on a formal level for expressive and communicative purposes. This goal is central in the theatrical performance *Stomp,* created in 1988 by a group of young English and American artists. The show, lasting ninety minutes without interruption, is a crescendo of vocal and mechanical sounds without words or melody. The rhythm is produced by eight musicians and dancers who use everyday objects, from brooms, to match-boxes, to trash cans, accompanying the percussions with syncopated foot-work. On the stage, everyday objects become a pretext for producing noises that are brought to the extreme among liberating cries, all within an accelerating rhythmic pattern that associates the entire process to the verticality of male orgasm. The sounds range from the delicate rustling of a piece of cloth to the clang of petrol drums, and the whole bears witness to the aggressive currents that everyday life is caught in. Other extreme representations of social violence are found in movies like Oliver Stone's *Natural Born Killers,* where this aspect is taken to the limit. Ethan and Joel Cohen's *Fargo,* which responds to the explosions of metropolitan violence in *Pulp Fiction,* is gratuitous to the point of being comic, with the atrocity of a pointless crime perpetrated in provincial America and solved by a pregnant woman cop.

On the one hand, these products denounce an ominous trend in our lives, but on the other hand, they are in themselves an alarming instance of how pervasive this phenomenon has become. It cannot be denied in fact that the subaltern cultures and minorities experience aspects of violence that each one of us experiences in everyday life. However, to state that teenage groups, metropolitan gangs, or even the more radical fringes of given minorities are again indiscriminately privileging the use of violence as a natural element of their identity and of their relationship to society would be a gross mistake. Perhaps the opposite is true. Their struggle is the struggle to escape the need for identity violently imposed on them by the dominant culture; they are withdrawing from the violence of this process. The rage produced by exclusion can therefore be transformed into a new way of being together, creating collectivities bound by common goals rather than by ethnic or racial ties, or it can finally be directed toward ritualized fantasies that constitute the postmodern modes of conceptualizing artistic movements. All these possibilities are products of the awareness that it is no longer possible to assert one's identity as the location of one's origin to be marked off in a material and cultural sense. There are presences, such as Deleuze and Guattari's nomadic avant-gardes or Monique Wittig's warring Amazons, forms of mobilization and aggressive collective fronts, which have undergone a complete process of *disidentification.* The passages in Wittig's *Les Guerrillerres* and the poems in Audré Lorde's *Black Unicorn* are lyrical manifestoes that are less intended to provoke than to empower, to violently activate nonviolent and noncategorical counter-formations. For Deleuze and Guattari these works trace creative escape routes within the confines where people move. For Wittig, who challenges the poetic display of violence in Frantz Fanon's *uprising,* the artistic expressions in dance and theater are what turns the violence of the oppressed, in a cultural and lyrical context, into the central element of the transformation process. In this sense, the need to position oneself coincides with the awareness that being "out of place" and "out of bounds" is a fundamental aspect of our lives.

Outlandishness

> *In my life I have never loved any people or collectivity, neither the German people, nor the French, nor the American, not the working class, nor anything of this type. The only type of love that I know and that I believe in is the love for an individual. Love for the Jewish people would seem to me to be suspicious since I am a Jew. The specific Jewish humanity,* in the name *of losing your world, was constantly something of great beauty. Being-outside-all-the social-ties, this is a total lack of prejudice, which I experienced with my mother who also "applied" it to the Jewish community.*
>
> —Hanna Arendt
> *The Mother Tongue (La Lingua Materna)*[1]

THE THEMES OF HYBRIDITY AND DISPLACEMENT ARE CENTRAL IN POST-colonial literature, the literature of those countries and subjects that have been colonized by the Western world and have sought and are still seeking forms of resistance to the domination by Western social and narrative categories, as well as modes of cultural reconstruction that would help to overcome that domination. Of course, this includes a broad range of positions and theoretical analyses produced by intellectuals from Jamaica, India, Africa, the Middle East, Asia, Australia, South America, etc., which are expressive of different attitudes toward the various forms of colonialism that were implanted in those countries.

The value of postcolonial discourse lies in the fact that it provides a methodology incorporating both similarity and difference: the similarity of the political and historical pressure on non-European societies coupled with the plurality of effects and cultural responses that this pressure has produced. The idea of origin, of authenticity, is no longer important, as a profound intricate juxtaposition of different cultures makes a distinction between them impossible, nullifying the concept of ethnic identity. In many cases, the dominant colonial culture becomes so intimately interconnected with the culture of the colonized that any effort to reclaim an origin or search for an authenticity is bound to fail. The rigid dualistic separation of the self and the other—of the "bourgeois" Robinson

Crusoe and the "noble savage" Friday—is undermined by the ambivalence of mobile subjects. Focusing exclusively on the rapacity of colonial empires would foster the belief that the dominant culture has completely prevailed, while preserving all its purity, thus making its power much more absolute and univocal than it actually is. It would also fail to problematize past and present forms of resistance, presenting them in purely binary terms such as center vs. margins, self vs. other, colonizer vs. the colonized, ignoring what Sara Suleri calls the "peculiar intimacy" of the colonizer and the people colonized. The power of subcultures lies in their hybridity. As Sara Suleri writes in reference to the dominion of the British empire and to postcolonial strategies for overcoming it:

> The necessary intimacies that obtain between rulers and ruled create a counter-culture not always explicable in terms of an allegory of the otherness [. . .]. Rather than examine a binary rigidity between those terms—which is an inherently Eurocentric strategy—this critical field would be better served if it sought to break down the fixity of the dividing lines between domination and subordination and if it further questioned the psychic disempowerement signified by colonial encounter [. . .]. If the paradigm of master and victim is to be read in terms of its availability to the histories of colonialism and the concomitant narratives, then its re-reading as a figure of colonial intimacy—as an interruption in traditional interpretations of imperial power—must necessarily generate a discursive guilt at the heart of the idiom of English India. Its troubled confluence of colony, culture, and nation lends a retroactive migrancy to the fact of imperialism itself, causing a figure like Kipling's Ahab to recognize that narration occurs to confirm the precariousness of power.[2]

The problem many postcolonial subcultures face is that of reacting and responding to the violence of colonialism without espousing its methods and value system. This problem has been hotly debated especially among feminists, who link the racial problem with that of gender. This debate has produced sophisticated theories but also violent polemics, especially when feminists belonging to colonial countries have accused Western feminism of being an instrument of a new colonization, insofar as it ignores the often aberrant developments that have occurred in certain postcolonial societies. Some authors have therefore claimed the peculiarity of the feminism of colonized countries and have criticized the interpretation of female marginality in third-world countries produced by Western feminism as excessively unitary and monolithic. Chandra Mohanty, for example, has accused Western feminism of presenting an essentialist view of the condition of women in colonial countries. Black feminism in Western countries, too, is accused of turning "direct experience" into a theoretical farce, unable to produce an adequate response to the violence that women are subject to in postcolonial societies. In this regard, Sara Suleri sees the elaborations of Trinh T. Minh-ha and bell hooks as incapable of furnishing, within feminist postcolonial critical theory, concrete answers to the crude "realism" of laws existent in countries such as Pakistan, where women are often mere objects of rape and other atrocities.

It is interesting to note that the work of Trinh T. Minh-ha has contributed to defining feminism and postcolonial theory as characterized by contradictions, interstices, and unclear, indefinable spaces. In addressing the theme of the *inappropriate/d other,* the representation of postcolonial women in an intermediate and yet real space *within the borders of their homeland,* contributes certainly to the reorganization and redescription of situational or experiential politics and those "situated knowledges" discussed by Donna Haraway. This space is not defined simply in terms of the overcoming of the fundamental binarism of center and margin, but also as the abandonment of authenticity as a reaction to the loss of possible identification of one's self. This continuous search for the self becomes a trap that we fall into. The center is itself a margin. As Trinh T. Minh-ha writes:

> Not foreigner, yet foreign. At times rejected by her own community, other times needfully retrieved, she is both useful and useless. . . . This shuttling in-between frontiers is a working out of and an appeal to another sensibility, another consciousness of the condition of marginality: that in which marginality is the condition of the center[. . .]. "I" is not unitary, culture has never been monolithic, and is always more or less in relation to a judging subject. Differences do not only exist between outsider and insider—two entities—; they are also at work within the outsider or the insider—a single entity.[3]

Trinh T. Minh-ha is aware of the problem summarized in Audré Lorde's expression "the masters' tools will never dismantle the masters' house." She is aware of the risk that the adoption of the theoretical instruments of patriarchy may make the dismantling of patriarchal culture impossible and could lead to new forms of marginalization. She is constantly torn between the desire for authenticity, the desire for the roots that would provide a sense of direction, and the sense of estrangement that comes from a dismembered self. Perhaps these difficulties seem less overwhelming once she distinguishes between difference, reduced to identity-authenticity and critical difference within oneself. Trinh T. Minh-ha concludes that any process of decolonization that seeks to eliminate racism and sexism must have as a reference point the women's culture and movement.

The theme of hybridity and displacement has been discussed by two intellectuals of Indian origin: Gayatri Chakravorty Spivak and Homi Bhabha, who have radically emphasized the closeness of the colonized and the colonizing subject, turning it into the central aspect of their theoretical analysis even while resisting the lure of merely ideological positions. Spivak and Bhabha move within a European theoretical framework and are inspired by the principle theorized by Fanon that the process of decolonization must consist first and foremost in forms of resistance and opposition to domination. The conclusions reached by Gayatri Chakravorty Spivak, famous for having criticized European feminism, accusing it of having constructed an essentialist notion of woman, are deeply pessimistic, leaving little hope for any positive solution to the problem of decolonization. She wonders, for example, whether, in the light of its hybrid identity, it is at all possible to speak of the postcolonial subject without falling victim once again to forms of essentialism that deny the heterogeneity that characterizes subalternity.

Is it really possible—Spivak asks—and is it really necessary to write a historiography of subalternity? Is not the very search for the place whence this subject could speak a contradiction in terms? It is therefore impossible for any scholar to write such a history without freezing it in an object of investigation, or worse yet, in a model to imitate. So it would seem, according to Spivak, when one observes the female subject. When race and class differences are subsumed in the relation between women and silence, they cancel each other as fundamental components of the same entity. Spivak's conclusions are inspired by a radical skepticism motivated, in her opinion, by the awareness that it is impossible to express the complex articulation of the subaltern subject without unwittingly contributing to the improvement of the colonial system that one wishes to destroy. Writes Spivak: "Subaltern historiography must confront the impossibility of such gestures. The narrow epistemic violence of imperialism gives us an imperfect allegory of the general violence that is the possibility of an episteme [. . .] . If, in the context of colonial production the subaltern has no history and cannot speak, the subaltern as female is even more deeply in shadow[. . .] .The postcolonial intellectuals learn that their privilege is their loss. In this they are the paradigm of the intellectuals."[4]

To Spivak's uncompromising rejection of the possibility of a space where the "colonial" may be reinscribed in history thanks to the intervention of deconstructive practices enacted by postcolonial intellectuals, Bhabha answers with recurring episodes of transgression enacted by the dominated ones within and against postcolonial discourse. Bhabha, too, reacts, in the wake of the positions outlined by Said in *Orientalism,* to the monolithic representation of the Other as passive Difference and, like Spivak and Suleri, rejects all forms of essentialism. The dominant narrative reveals contradictory articulations, a wide range of stereotypes and aporetical discrepancies in the assignment of fixed positions to the colonial subject within the colonialist text. From this perspective, the colonial subject discovers that the fundamental characteristic of the colonial text and culture resides precisely in this hybridity, so that when he/she proceeds to rewrite his/her history, the result is no longer a copy of the original but something qualitatively different, where errors of reading and interpretation expose the uncertainties of the colonial text itself and undermine its authority. In doing this, the colonial reappropriates the text and this action becomes an act of subversive opposition to the culture of authenticity. The possibility of the subaltern subject to speak exists when the mediation enacted through the mimicry and parody of the dominant discourse subvert and threaten the authority within whose boundaries it is necessarily born. And the fact that this resistance can be developed within the area of mimicry highlights the necessarily hybrid condition of colonial societies. "The place of difference and otherness," writes Bhabha, "or the space of the adversarial, within such a system of 'disposal' as I've proposed, is never entirely on the outside or implacably oppositional."[5]

Hybridity becomes a distinctive sign of colonial power as well as of its production. Thus a new form of subversion arises based on the uncertainty that transforms the conditions of dominant discourse that lays the foundation for action. This is the distinctive sign of postcolonial cultures through which they express their presence.

The Jamaican, Edward Kamau Brathwaite, calls this process *Creolization,* referring to the cultural process of hybridization that characterized Creole society, i.e., a society where the slaves were imported to work the plantations under the surveillance of people of European origin. The condition of displacement affects both sides of binarisms such as black/white or master/slave and intersects other traditions and ethnic groups. These dualisms become meaningless. In fact, the process of ethnic and cultural juxtaposition affects all local subjects, who, entering into contact, render the concept of authenticity meaningless. Braithwaite's notion of *Creolization* is based on the notion of a social and cultural *continuum* within which, as in Jamaica, at least four layers of intermingled traditions existed overlapping one with the other. From its variegated cultural starting point, the Caribbean people tend toward specific directions, positions, assumptions, and ideals. "But nothing is really fixed and monolithic. Although there is white/brown/black, there are infinite possibilities within these distinctions and many ways of asserting identity."[6]

The fluidity that characterizes the search for postcolonial identity is a recurring feature of those cultures which, rather than emphasizing the drama of the loss of authenticity, live and proliferate in a mutual, continuous and protean development. In Jamaica, Nigeria, and many parts of Africa, as witnessed by Karin Barber, for example, this hybridity manifests itself through the embodiment of elements of written culture in the oral tradition.

Certainly, it is not easy to avoid the sense of loneliness and estrangement that this process of hybridization can produce. The result is often suffering, depression, and a sense of impotence deriving from the inability to identify one's identity and that of others, an unnerving oscillation between the desire to locate oneself within known parameters and the impossibility of belonging to any particular place. This is the "mestizo" mental state that on the one hand is characterized by insecurity and on the other opens up the possibility of venturing toward the unknown. This is the melancholy that characterizes writers such as V. S. Naipaul, born in Trinidad of a Hindu family and educated in England, who bears witness to the sense of displacement typical of this literature through an aristocratic detachment and the metaphor of foreignness. Naipaul realizes he is out of place, in the condition he defines as "homelessness." Yet, this condition is also a privileged one, allowing him to realize the meaninglessness of the search for origins. It is this "surreal" *foreignness* in which the protagonist of Salman Rushdie's *The Moor's Last Sigh* moves. The character is forced by circumstances to leave India, his mother country, and enter a world that is completely unknown to him, making him realize that he likewise knows nothing about himself and his family. At the end of this journey and of his brief life, the character, part of an unfortunate and dramatic family saga, draws a parallel between personal history and writing, concluding that his story bears witness to our most important and significant need, that of "transgressing frontiers and abandoning the boundaries of the self."

In a similar fashion, Anita Desai takes this conclusion to the extreme when, in her splendid novel *Baumgartner's Bombay,* she speaks about the *outlandishness* of her protagonist Hugo Baumgartner. "Outlandishness," even more than Naipaul's "homelessness" and Rushdie's "foreignness," indicates the sense of being foreign even to one's own self, of hovering over the edge of mental pathology. Desai's main character, a Jewish child, comes from Germany, the heart of European colonialism, where he is a pariah, the lower rung in the ethnic-social ladder of a country caught in the frenzy of anti-Semitism. He is forced to flee, emigrating in order to save himself from Nazi persecution. His lot is that of the foreigner in all the countries and cultures he moves in: in Germany because he is Jewish, in India because he is neither British nor Indian. *Firanghi* is his condition in the Indian language: "Accepting but not being accepted; that was the story of his life; the one thread which ran through it all. In Germany he had been dark—his darkness had marked him the Jew, *der Jude.* In India he was fair and that marked him the *firanghi.* In both lands, the unacceptable."[7]

But the character is also a marginalized figure who leads a lonely and alienated life "without family or mother country."[8] For him, silence is the natural condition in an estranged life lived at the boundaries of the flooding of the self. He envies "the simplicity, the absence of choice and history" of the people who inhabit the slum where he also lives and compares their lives to his life, always confined in what he symbolically defines as the "barbed-wire" of his unhappy conscience: the obligation to choose that follows from his condition of not belonging. The past always reemerges from the depths of the unconscious where memory becomes bits of vital matter to hold on to in the moments of loneliness. The tragedy of his life is represented precisely by his awareness that his ignorance, his foreignness, his silence, his *outlandishness,* will never be safe from the reappropriations of history. His death at the hands of another firanghi from his same world and past represents the historical nemesis in the saga of this survivor of the nightmare of historical rigidity.

Yet, from a different perspective, the hybrid condition also offers the possibility of breaking the barriers of time and space, revealing the tremendous power of outlandishness. This is the case of Hannah Easton, the main character in the novel *Holder of the World* by Bharati Mukherjee. Like Desai, Hannah, too, belongs to the Western world and has a subaltern position, being a woman. Yet, she turns her nonbelonging into an instrument of wonder, freedom, and joy, which allows her to look back upon the past not with nostalgia but with a sense of estrangement; in other words, outlandishness. It is not by chance that Mukherjee's character is a woman. In recent times, feminism and postcolonial studies have developed along similar lines, both definitely rejecting a mere reversal of positions.

These issues have come increasingly to the forefront in the United States where the migratory movement from excolonies is constantly on the rise and where the majority of the above cited postcolonial intellectuals live, work (usually in academia), and publish in English.

For example, the media have produced a large number of movies, especially by groups of intellectuals and artists, that are more politically engaged and more sensitive to cultural and social changes. This is the case of *Smoke* and *Blue in the Face,* two movies, both by Wayne Wang and Paul Auster, that were released in quick succession and are both centered around a small tobacco shop in Brooklyn, where shopkeeper, Auggie (Harvey Keitel), functions as the *trait-de-union* among the various characters that move in and out of his shop, each with his own specific story and different ethnic and social background. In the second movie, where famous artists like Lou Reed, Jim Jarmusch, Lily Tomlin, and Madonna make an appearance, often in marginal roles, the story is shifted to the ethnic, cultural composition of Brooklyn rather than individual stories. Thus characters who are the real-life owners of the shops next to Auggie's or simple bystanders stand up in front of the camera and enumerate the percentages of the various ethnic minorities that live in the neighborhood, celebrating the hybridity of cultural identities which thus become the privileged subject of the images that we see. The young black who comes into Auggie's shop trying to sell phony brand name wrist watches is surprised and perplexed when he meets another black with an Italian last name who indeed defines himself as Italian. A playful discussion on the subject of black identity follows and, while the black youth fails to be convinced that the other is an Italian, it does lead to an agreement among all the bystanders that there is no problem of authenticity, but only individual ways of experiencing one's identity, something that goes beyond the color of the skin and other codified notions of belonging. At the end of the movie we meet the same black man again, conveniently transvested in an elegant white suit trying to fake a Spanish accent in order to work his same con game. He is immediately recognized by the same Italian black he talked to the first time and there follows an amusing debate on the exhilarating, liberating effect of faking one's identity and playing games with one's self and with others. The first movie, *Smoke,* has a more conventionally structured story line, centered on a writer (William Hurt) and his relation with Auggie and with a young black who has run away from home, but, like its sequel, it deals with the problem of hybrid identities and of the lack of roots that increasingly characterizes modern society. This is also the central theme in the problematic conclusion of the movie, when Auggie tells the writer, who is stuck without a subject for his next book, a story which we have no way of knowing is true or false. The starting point is Auggie finding a wallet containing the photo of a young black with his grandmother. It is Christmas and Auggie decides to visit the old lady to bring her back the photo of her grandson, who has ended up in jail. But the old lady lives alone, is blind, and believes or wishes to believe that Auggie is her grandson. Auggie plays along, although he is convinced that the woman knows perfectly well that he is a stranger. In a corner, Auggie notices a heap of cameras, and at the end of the day he steals one. Afterwards, he engages in his photographic project, which consists in taking a picture outside his shop every day, at the same time and from the same angle. The photos illustrate a succession of different skin colors, different faces, different stories that juxtapose and mingle against the same background. This is Auggie's way of showing the passing time and of representing memory. The end of the movie marks a beginning, i.e., the beginning of a story; we will never know whether it is the original, authentic one, or a fabrication. A close-up of Auggie's smiling face ends the movie. Irony becomes the fundamental instrument for undermining the seriousness and purity of origin and memory.

Irony

It is in reality a serious study to learn to temper, regulate that humor which nature has given us, as a more lenitive remedy against vice, and a kind of specific against superstition and melancholy delusions. There is a great difference between seeking how to raise a laugh from everything, and seeking in every thing what justly may be laughed at . . . There fore it is the hardest thing in the world to deny, fair Honestly, the use of this weapon, which can never bear an edge against herself and bears nothing against every thing contrary.

—Anthony Ashley Cooper, Third Earl of Shaftesbury, *Characteristics of Men, Manners, Opinions, Times with a Collection of Letters* (1711)[1]

AT THE BEGINNING OF HER "CYBORG MANIFESTO," DONNA HARAWAY DEscribes the importance that the element of irony has in her theoretical and political construction, whose final product is nothing but the cyborg:

> This chapter is an effort to build an *ironic* [the italics are the author's] political myth faithful to feminism, socialism and materialism. Perhaps more faithful as blasphemy is faithful, than as a reverent worship and identification. Blasphemy has always seemed to require taking things very seriously. I know no better stance to adopt from within the secular-religious, evangelical traditions of United States politics, including the politics of socialist feminism.[. . .] Irony is about contradictions that do not resolve into larger wholes, even dialectically, about the tension of holding incompatible things together because both or all are necessary and true. Irony is about humor and serious play. It is also a rhetorical strategy and a political method [. . .]. At the centre of my ironic faith, my blasphemy is the image of the cyborg.[2]

It is precisely in this perspective that irony becomes for me an essential moment in the construction of disidentification techniques. Not taking oneself seriously, playing with one's roles and with one's identity is essential because it provides the necessary detachment toward that systematic body of beliefs and values in which we often find ourselves trapped. To play means, aside from definitions that now seem banal and can be taken for granted, at least formally, to play with the authority of Reason and

Truth, assuming there is one, none, and/or a thousand. It means falsifying origins, living in continuous contact with paradox, stimulating the imagination, inventing and reinventing oneself by narrating stories, the truth of which is irrelevant. In short, it means going in a direction that is completely opposite to the one chosen and propagated, like an infectious disease, by philosophy, which has turned the search for truth and the adherence to the laws of reason into its crucial ontological goal. *Cheating* becomes essential, at least in relation to the truth of Origin, belonging, identity. There is no need for "objective" proofs or extenuating legitimization. We can free the storyteller within each one of us and express the creativity that would return to us the multifaceted dimension that we have lost. Telling a story made up of gaps and errors, which alter the original and official version, undermines the authority of the dominant narrative that created it and the language through which it expressed itself. It is the form of narrating and singing stories adopted by Laurie Anderson, who uses irony as a fundamental element in the articulation of her musical pieces and her relationship to language. The theme of the relation between music and word is certainly not new in the American culture, and the *Harlem Renaissance* is one of the crucial moments in its history. From then up to the *beat generation,* which rediscovered jazz, turning it into the model for a new literary style, artists such as Duke Ellington, Charlie Mingus, John Coltrane, and the great Billie Holiday have inspired lyrical poetry. They showed the close connection between these two artistic forms, which has often been translated into active collaboration between poets and musicians. Thus, LeRoy Jones has studied the relationship between the rhythm of poetry and jazz. Steve Lacey, who collaborated, among others, with William Burroughs, dedicated his 1986 LP *Condor* to poetry, turning detachment into a form of ironic *estrangement,* which emphasizes the technical construction of this musical creation. Laurie Anderson, too, albeit in a completely different musical genre, explores these experiences, on the one hand giving visibility to the relationship between word and musical language, and on the other demonstrating its constructiveness as an element that reveals the impossibility of establishing clearly defined boundaries between real-life experiences and artistic forms. This is the ironic surrealism of the Burroughs-like composition *Language is a Virus,* found in the CD, *Home of the Brave: A Film by Laurie Anderson,* where sometimes tribal music, constantly underscored by a saxophone that modulates the human voice, is associated with a language contaminated by performance and image. Just like a virus, language infects the cells that govern communication between human beings. More than a vehicle of spirituality and expression of the materiality of bodies, it becomes a dangerous instrument of indifference, fruit of a fixed and incommunicable knowledge, which contaminates the consumerist world we live in. The obsessive division of labor, which dominates all the productive sectors, and the extreme specialization of roles in the private sphere and in the professions have blocked all the possibilities for mobility and transformation in individuals and in the work force. They have also contributed in a fundamental way to the suppression of multiplicity, but they also have indirectly opened "black holes" in which the role of the margin is essential. The story, therefore, must take place within the form of the dominant narrative, moving between the spaces it creates and defines and the spaces it leaves out, the unseen spaces, the *space off,* which represent the privileged terrain of this subalternity. Moving continuously between these two spaces not only allows us to escape a one-way trajectory, but also lightens the burden of being alternative, offering the possibilities of retelling stories different from the original, which no longer have any relation to the original. Being constantly *elsewhere,* marginalized and subaltern subjects, continually forces us to give attention and take care of our fellow "navigators" in a context of complete extraneity to all affiliations. As an Italian, the first example that comes to my mind when I think of the possibility of rediscovering our multidimensionality and creativity as individuals is the original experiment of Radio Alice in Bologna, at the end of the 1970s. Its creator, Bifo, was responsible for the formation of an "alternative" group of young people of proletarian extraction, who used irony and paradox as its fundamental tools for narration and self-narration, of living, and of escaping the forms of genocide both open and hidden that the Italian political leaders, the institutional left-wing more than others, enacted during the late 1970s and the 1980s. The originality of this experiment consisted precisely in the ironic and irreverent use of the same propaganda medium that Fascism had used to gain a wide-ranging consensus: the radio. It is the same mechanism that characterizes the recent collection of short stories by Salman Rushdie *East, West.* The author of *Satanic Verses,* using the same cultural tools and references used to construct stereotyped images of the East and the West, which in this case, India and England are the privileged signifiers, destroys all the myths on which the presumed authenticity of their representation is based. Thus, in the case of the West, to ridicule Prince Hamlet and the pale Ophelia, or figures like Christopher Columbus and Queen Isabella, tied to the discovery of the New World, he reshapes them, destroying their sacred symbolical function, performing a "sacrilegious" act of fierce irony, which undermines the authenticity of those myths. As for Eastern culture, and specifically Indian culture, to ridicule England and Islamic religion, two sacred metaphors of that world, is equivalent to undermining the legendary solidity of dominant traditions. Thus, in the first story, bearing the significant title *Good Advice is Rarer than Rubies,* Rushdie speaks about the meeting of a young woman, who apparently wishes to emigrate to England, with an old schemer, who, attracted by her beauty, advises her on how to answer the questions of the British consulate in order to obtain a passport. Without offering any explanation, the woman answers in precisely the opposite way and remains in the small town where she lives and works. In another story, Rushdie again satirizes, as in his most famous work, Islamic superstition and integralism. In *The Prophet's Hair,* the relic represented by the hair of a Muslim prophet brings great misfortune to a professional money lender, who, after having illicitly appropriated it, is subject to a sort of curse, and begins to orthodoxly practice Islamic law, oppressing his entire family. His children are forced to hire a professional thief to have him steal the relic from their house and return it to the mosque where it belongs. But it is too late and the little but powerful hair has already wrought its effect, bringing misfortune to all that have come in contact with it. In the last story *East, West,* which gives the collection its title, Rushdie shows how the meeting of the two worlds produces characters that inhabit a twilight zone, where nationalities and identities intermingle and confuse themselves in unpredictable and unforeseen ways: they are hybrids drifting away. Thus, Rushdie tells the story of two Indian friends who meet again in England where they are both diplomats and who, by continuing to act out the *Star Trek* fantasies of their youth, end up being involved in international terrorist plots in their own native country, which by now is autonomously producing those same monstrous conspiracies of which it was wont to accuse England, the country that had oppressed and depredated it. Then comes a subtle and bitter story, *The Harmony of the Spheres,* in which the Indian protagonist—after the suicide of a British friend in Wales, following a long and serious mental infirmity—is asked to read the notes on his friend's "mad" erotic fantasies in which the protagonist's wife played a major role. He finally discovers that the fantasies were not the product of mental disorder, but the plain and simple truth.

All the stories contained in Rushdie's book are based on a sophisticated and amused irony, and on extensive punning, which, as in *The Moor's Last Sigh,* often extend to the character's names. Moor, for example besides the obvious meaning, also refers to "moorings," as if the last sigh of the protagonist, whose existential tragedy is the traumatic break with his mother, refers to the end of stability, not only of the culture associated with the Islamic world and religion, but also of the Oedipal relationship, whose discovery has not been limited to the Western world, infecting the Eastern one, as well. The Moor, the "narrator/narratee," descending on one side from the Portuguese family de Gama, and on the other, from the Jewish family of Zogoiby, lives in a world of the past, represented by India of the twentieth century. In the remaining part of his life, all that is left to him is the realization that he is a "as jetsam and located in an environment of broken and discarded objects, many of which were 'found' items, pieces of crates or vanaspati tins that were fixed to the surface of the work and painted over."[3] Like words, any notion of "authentic" identity is subject to playful deconstruction. This is symbolized by his young fiancée, Uma, whom he loves above all, and who dies in his place by mistake, on account of an involved series of events produced by passionate and material conflicts. Subsequently, we discover that the poison that killed her had been prepared by her but intended for the Moor. Her identity—Rushdie suggests—is confused, indistinct, "independent of these performances and this existential confusion had begun to spread beyond the borders of her own self and to infect like a disease all those with whom she came into contact."[4] Uma lies because she does not grasp the significance and importance of truth in a world like India, subject to a sort of "cosmopolitan Westoxication," intoxication from the West, which prevents it from clearly establishing the boundaries of identity and values to the point that it is impossible to establish original places. The triumph of hybridity casts doubt on the legitimacy of knowledge and of individual and social morals. By breaking the boundary between what is true and what is false, what is good and what is evil, it undermines any normative stability of these concepts, as if they were ready-to-use cans.

This "anarchy" of the self has been discussed by Hakim Bey in his now famous *T.A.Z. The Temporary Autonomous Zone: Ontological Anarchy, Poetic Terrorism,* where, rejecting revolution as a too visible and identifiable means of social and personal transformation, he proposes forms of subversiveness based on the principle of mobility and disappearance. Revolution is transformed from *tocsin* to *toxin,* i.e., a warning bell announcing the destruction of the establishment, transforming into a toxin, a poison that taints society with obsessive fixation on power and State. "Why *bother* to confront a 'power' which has lost all meaning and becomes sheer Simulation?" asks Bey.[5] Through the hybrid symbol of pirates who are not represented by official history, except in certain small and unknown museums in the Caribbean, Bey suggests forms of tactic *situationism* that mutates the positioning *somewhere* (precisely like the cyborgs, who disappear after having hit their target) into an unstable, agile, and ironic instrument of transformation. Central to Bey's formulation are the technological and artistic elements. Technology opens spaces of counterpower, temporarily coalesced in mobile organizations which the Tazs, the "temporary autonomous zones," exploit through a disappearance tactic. The avoidance of all forms of *mediation,* for Bey, is achieved through the performance of sudden acts of informatic "hacking" moments. These are moments of poetic fantasy, guaranteeing the democratic structure of information through horizontal communicative exchange, forms of *counter-Net* and the *Web.* These become weapons of democracy, a sixth sense that forces us to reconsider our image, a sort of reconstruction of the self starting from the oneself. As Maurizio Viano notes, Tazs call our attention to a reconsideration of our body chemistry with which we constantly interact through interfaces such as food, smoke, chemical substances, or anything that we introduce in our body, as well as through other bodies, being of other species, or technology. All this brings about a "harmony, a law of its own," which gives embodiment the meaning "to subsume in our body, but also to embody ourselves, to be one body with another through love, through sex [. . .] a love that must not, in heterocratic forms, associate people of opposite sex, or, in humanistic form, associate people of the same human species."[6] Thus it is possible to interface with chemical substances, animals, or machines. It is necessary, in other words, to pay attention to a body chemistry that goes beyond the "natural" relation between beings of different sex or of the same species, overcoming the materiality of bodies and revealing their porosity and constructiveness. I do not mean to propose ideas of perfection and of aseptic posthuman worlds where the corruptibility of the body no longer exists and the expansion of the mind's capacity for knowledge is boundless. On the contrary I mean to challenge the normative boundaries that our body and our self has accustomed itself to and whose destruction it usually resists, through a panic-depressive reaction. Furthermore, it is necessary to remove this encounter from the abnormal world of terminal illness and substance abuse (where people feel isolated and experience the loneliness and tragedy of such conditions) and to bring it into our daily lives, in order, on the one hand, to increase our expressive capacities, and, on the other, to redefine "health" and "normality" in different terms. Even in this case, however, we are dealing with a momentary recomposition, the product of unstable mediations, which are temporary like the utopias of pirates, for whom, as Bey notes, true 'republics' were their ships, which sailed under Articles. The shore enclaves usually had no law at all."[7] It is the metaphor of movement under the form of *Indianness,* which, as Bey notes, represented the "dream" of withdrawing *par excellence* from the slavery of all dominant cultures, suggesting images of eroticism, sexuality, and "denudation of one's self." Indianness was an ethnic label invented by white culture to catalogue the native people of North America, endowed with extremely diversified traditions and cultures. Their only common elements were the fact of being "savages" and of having been subjugated by "civilized" colonizers. Indianness, as a representation of difference and alterity, also brings to the foreground the role played by women in those societies, which had already aroused the interest of Lafiteau in the eighteenth century. As Paola Bora observes, this Jesuit, in many ways the precursor of modern ethnology, focuses on the matrilinearity that characterizes these social groups, making it into a "point of *maximum diversity* from the principles of descendancy and family organization that had been taken to be universal."[8] The fact of being an anthropological eccentricity, a representation of foreignness to official history, the permanent condition of an existential *elsewhere,* half-way between a subaltern culture confined to the marginal spaces of reservations within the territory of the United States and the culture of the pale faces. Finally, a narrative based on an oral tradition, which, in nomadic contexts, is ironically situated each time *somewhere else,* in different social and historical locations, which displace those of the dominant written interpretation; all these make Indianness into an essential element for the understanding of *passing.* The figures of native American culture, reflecting and communicating the virus of hybridity, of nomadism, of the crossing of the boundaries of affiliation, and of language, within the context of the reprogramming of knowledge and sentient horizons, represent par excellence, that magical and ironic aura intimately connected with the restructuring of our individual selves. The time-lag that suspends their culture is constantly displaced within official history; the *rage* that the human zoo of the reservation, which appears daily, offers to our eyes without ever identifying them, and the outlandishness of belonging prevents any form of protective cataloging, the sort used for species in danger of extinction, from being applied to them by "white" culture. *Irony,* the central element of this *oral* cultural tradition and the privileged tool of its situated narrative and history, allows it to evade the homogenous power of the dominant *written* culture, becoming a subversive and disquieting medium of communication and human interaction. Alan Velie, in his *Four American*

Indian Literary Masters, highlights the importance of irony in native American literature. Velie is the first intellectual to reject the attitude of investigation and control that dominates American and Western culture, which usually manifests itself in written social sciences, especially in regard to this typically oral culture.

Indian tribes have always been represented as tragic archetypes, never as comic or ironic, whether in the narratives written by white historians, in Hollywood movies, or in the statements produced by radical intellectuals or artists who have espoused the cause of a people who are prisoners in their own country.

On the contrary, there is a typical character in native American literature who is the depositary of irony: the "trickster figure." According to Velie, he is the most important mythical figure for most tribes. Significantly, he/she is one of the most important figures in contemporary native American novels. According to Gerald Vizenor, this figure is "androgynous, a comic healer, a liberator in literature; the *whole figuration* that ties the unconscious to social experience. The *trickster* sign is communal, an erotic shimmer in oral traditions."[9]

Who better than Native Americans, whose original white appellation "Indian" (derived from Columbus's well-known mistake), is in itself the simulation of how an absence can play with the history of origins that never existed? The existence of a *trickster* hermeneutics represents, thus, the interpretation of simulations in the creation of a literature in which the irony of descendance and the themes of transformation in Native American oral stories represent a form of liberation from the shackles imposed by the conscience of pale faces, who have erected their own history upon it. Furthermore, these stories become representative of the peculiar signifier of Indianness, a myth invented by white culture to celebrate its purity and innocence. This hermeneutics of liberation shows a sense of humor that denies the existence of the tragic dimension as a stereotype and an interpretative key of Native American culture. Post-Indian warriors then, through their trickster stories, according to Vizenor, displace the centrality of Western "pale face" narrative insofar as "with imagination and the performance of new stories, they manifest manners and overcome the written simulations and 'authentic' representations of tribes in the literature of dominance."[10] The Native American chief Russell Means, who along with other chiefs of the Movement of Native Americans sat for Andy Warhol's portrait *American Indian,* which bore the caption "this is not an Indian," is an example of how this may function. The process of painting a portrait is the revelation of an absence;

the caption shows the existence of a form of discursive ambiguity in regards to the simulations and the sources of tribal identities. Is it really possible to speak of native American identity or is not its narration simply the projection of something that can exist only in the form of a linguistic denomination, created for the purpose of justifying performances conceived, acted out and written by dominant literature? The fact of having sat for a portrait bearing such a caption summarizes what Magritte wrote in his painting of a pipe: "Ceci n'est une pipe," where, as Foucault has noted in the essays of the same title, one perceives both the power of discourse to penetrate things, and the ambiguity of its power to negate and double.

II

Passing

Betraying Your Origins

PASSING IS THE TITLE OF A NOVEL BY THE AMERICAN WRITER NELLA Larsen, one of those intellectuals and artists who, during the 1920s, renovated black culture through jazz and literature, giving rise to the movement known as the *Harlem Renaissance.*

Larsen's *Passing,* written in 1929, tells the story of two women, Clare and Irene, who grow up together in the black ghetto of Chicago, lose touch, and casually meet again after several years. Notwithstanding their common background, there is a profound difference between them, which both inescapably divides and unites them, as we shall see. Clare has severed connections with her race, while Irene has remained faithful to her origins. Irene has left Chicago, married a doctor, and leads a relatively comfortable life in Harlem. Clare, too, is relatively well off, but is fairly reticent about her life, as she has taken advantage of her light skin to hide her black origins and marry a racist white man. This behavior was quite common at that time in the United States, especially in the South, where there were countless cases of racial hybridization because of slavery. The word used to describe the phenomenon of blacks who passed as whites was passing. It is from this word that Nella Larsen's book receives its title. The practice of passing was useful for avoiding racial discrimination and defending oneself from violence and persecution. At the same time, African Americans viewed those who *passed* as people who had betrayed their origins and given up on the fight against racial oppression.

The word also suggests a state of constant transition and, finally, a desire to withhold information, reminiscent of a poker game, when a player passes his/her hand without stating his/her position and the next move is left to other players. This leads to a complex, dangerous, but also intriguing situation, in which the other players must try to guess strategy and interpret behavior. Poker is not a gambler's game by coincidence. The other players are left to judge tactics and readability of behavior. In fact, poker is based on psychological acumen and player reactions. For this reason, it is said to be an intelligent game. By passing, the player postpones a commitment, ready to enter the game later on and place a bet.

Indeed, players often pass on a good hand in order to "raise" on somebody else's bet. Thus, a player will sometimes pass because of a bad hand and sometimes because he/she wants others to believe he/she has a bad hand. Yet, even with a bad hand, the player may decide later on to raise the ante. In the last two cases the player is bluffing, pretending to be something other than what he/she is. If the player passes with a good hand and no one else bets, he/she has lost a chance to bet, to make his/her voice heard. But if the strategy works, the adversary is caught off balance and forced to reconsider his former beliefs. What is intriguing in poker is the fact that although there are a number of rules, the game introduces a degree of flexibility through the possibility of bluffing. This tactical device allows the other players to be displaced. Games are usually based on rigid rules and conventions, and poker is no exception. But it contains an element that undermines the rigidity of its structure, allowing one to go against the rules and temporarily evade the win or lose logic typical of all games.

The title of my book is a product of a fascination with the possibility of subverting reality and bluffing offered by the practice of passing. Passing is possible, evidently, within a subaltern culture, when one wishes to avoid a direct confrontation with the dominant one. Its function is to prevent the subaltern culture from being completely legible. In this way it also challenges the dualistic and hierarchical structure of observation. A structure that, in the case of the white and black racial binarism, is centered on *white supremacy.* In contrast with the common view of this practice as a form of betrayal, I wish to emphasize its ability to evade the dominant culture, thus undermining its foundation and, especially, its authority. By passing, individuals travel through fluid, multifaceted phases of their existence, experiencing a multidimensional identity as a remedy against forms of indifference or hostility towards the other. Particles of matter wandering in space absorb or emit energy as soon as they come into contact with other particles. This is a nomadism of single individuals connecting through reciprocal protean relations, in which what is important is the real, emotional, desiring exchange, as opposed to the power relations. Passing, then, is a way of evading the increasingly categorical imperative of *belonging,* of affiliation, which attaches labels to everybody, assigning roles that soon turn out to be cages.[1] The violent reemergence of ethnic and religious affiliations in the heart of Europe is recent history, sad to say, and seems to know no boundaries. It crosses national borders, unsettling the old continent with tremors that we had hoped to be a thing of the past. It demands that we position ourselves, declare our origins, and prove our devotion to them lest we be accused of betrayal. This, indeed, is what happened to the former Yugoslavian film director Emir Kusturica, who directed his critique against the logic of belonging in his movie *Underground.* Using a style at once tragic and surreal, Kusturica shows how hatred of the enemy is learned, cultivated, and passed on from father to son, devastating and destroying people's lives. Through the reification of a paradox, it becomes literally impossible to distinguish the moon from the sun, to recognize the value of affection and human ties. It impedes from a literary point of view the celebration of a marriage on an island that, as is shown in the last scene of the film, has detached itself from the mainland and is adrift on a river. The people happily celebrating are serenely floating down a river, adrift, without a fixed destination or goal other than celebrating moments of common happiness. This is an image I would like to borrow to translate my concept of passing. Kusturica represents this separation as utopian, a dream ultimately destroyed by the reality of war, while for me it represents the hope in the possibility of a rebirth of nomadic communitarian feelings, of ties of solidarity and spirituality among people, and the reason for a new type of social commitment, different from the one we are forced to adhere to in our daily lives. Bifo talks about: "elective communities coinciding with a temporary and changeable system of interconnections. This creates the basis for a society of variable geometries and voluntary participation. This is a model of *virtual communities* [my emphasis], communities that one participates in but does not identify with, does not belong to, exchanging that which is useful and interesting to exchange, giving and receiving that which one desires to give and receive."[2]

Such communities are without territories, origin, or belonging. In them, individuals are more interested in the trip, in its significant intermediate stages, than in reaching at all costs a final destination.

A view that serves to undermine the paradigms of identity and politics, which from the ancient polis to the elaborations of the fathers of modern politics, from Machiavelli to recent Schmitt's theories of friend and enemy, had identified the ontological and essential goal of politics with the seizure of power. Yet, the present situation forces us to reconsider that final goal, precisely because the "official" and institutional form of power of modernity has not simply developed a few cracks in the façade of its representative capability, but is indeed rotten to the core. The disease has mined its fundamental structure, and new forms of political action have emerged that modernity had not foreseen and cannot account for. Representative democracy, the political form of modernity, appears incapable of expressing the complexity of the new social articulations that have developed within the cybernetic space of the digital world.

Feminist theories have contributed and continue to further destabilize the already tottering system. Along with the great migratory movements from the Third World to Europe and the United States, the role of women is the greatest factor in this epochal change of Western culture and society. Despite this, women's politics has a marginal position in this universe: at the very moment when the symbolic universe of men is undergoing an irreversible crisis, women have disappeared or are disappearing from the political scene. The incapability of politics to absorb social change and its tendency to reproduce itself in entirely male self-referential forms is visible in the continuous reterritorialization within which forms of monosexual narcissism, of which media politics is the most glamorous form (which I know is very apparent in Italy), reproduce and implode. For this reason, politics, along with the male symbolic universe on which it is based, is in a state of crisis. Those who, like women, have a history of exclusion, delay, and search for visibility, are advantaged because they can appear on the political stage with an uncommon trait: a ductile identity, which resists solidification and is opposed to male identity, which is entirely visible but in a state of irreversible crisis engendered by the tactile domination of new technologies. Thus, it is certainly important to have a common world to represent, but it is also necessary to reconsider what it means to belong to that world. This leads us to reflect upon the significance and importance of the formation of women's identity. It is the problem of what is to be done when the bill is presented for the proverbial pound of flesh. I have no ready-made answers or fast recipes for this. If we let ourselves be blackmailed by the immediacy of the problem, we must necessarily resort to limited and limiting solutions. If, on the other hand, we wish to avoid placing any boundary whatsoever on the profound autonomy of desire, the process becomes more complicated,[3] insofar as it must be considered in the context of the epochal mutation we are undergoing. This technological mutation questions the form of social relations and subjectivity associated with it.

"Technomediatic fluxes," as Bifo calls them, arrive from space, saturated by information circuits (cyberspace) and subcultural fluxes, travel through our mental sphere, interconnect and proceed to modify the collective image repertoire. Belonging, which, on the one hand, is related to the political forms through which subjectivity is represented and, on the other hand, to the most profound and intimate roots of the unconscious and therefore of individual identity, is a reaction against the massive invasion, which generates disorientation and depression in humans. Using the terminology of Deleuze and Guattari,[4] we may state that forms of *deterritorialization* determined by the panic caused by the incessant flow of neurons connected to the collective-social brain are followed by forms of *re-territorialization* that coalesce in belonging and the culture of original purity, for the purpose of achieving some kind of security. In reality, these defensive moves construct artificial origins for the purpose of recapturing lost certainties. Quite often this happens at the expense of individual passions and feelings. With this I do not mean to advocate distancing oneself from the social sphere or, in the case of women, engaging in forms of separatism. Nor do I wish to call for compromises of any kind. I simply wish to observe that there is an ontological aporia between the desire to encounter the other, to display and open to it one's "fluctuating" self—necessarily located outside the boundaries of institutional politics—and the desire to revise the same theoretical and material institutions of the very political asset that has excluded us.

It is this double bind, this ambiguity, that we need to take into account in our theoretical elaborations and political practice. The present transitional phase demands more than an immediate solution. Certainly, the problems of belonging are connected to vital issues such as identity and the unconscious, on the one hand, and political subjectivity and volition, on the other hand, and raise, therefore, crucial problems, which are the touchstones of our ability to survive this transition to the virtual era. The construction of these concepts must be revised or even abandoned. Therefore, it is important to respond to the challenge of "lightness" by starting from the concept of identity, which is intimately connected to the roots of the unconscious of each of us. This concept must be brought to a fluid state, because only in this way will it be possible to liberate energies that have been constrained for too long. However, this must be accomplished without obliterating the past and the phases that have determined it and without structuring and constraining the richness of our difference within "heavy" theoretical prison-houses. This is where the concept of passing becomes important, since, thanks to its flexibility, it allows us to revise the concept of belonging, intimately connected to the construction of the self and the other.

My analysis of Nella Larsen's novel, *Passing*—in which, in spite of the guilt feelings that lead to the tragic ending, alternative responses to the strictures of the ideology of racial integrity can be discerned—has precisely this purpose. This novel is a pretext for discussing the possibility of *disidentification,* which forces us to reconsider the limiting constructions of racial, ethnic, religious, or sexual identities, which we have inherited from the Enlightenment of the eighteenth century, the idealist and Marxist tradition of the nineteenth, and from all the more recent theoretical approaches that seek to solve the crisis of that type of reason through compromises and partial adjustments. Fortunately, this crisis is irreversible and must be celebrated as the moment when we can finally break out of the conceptual framework of the past, liberating ourselves from the limits of this thought structure.

Nella Larsen's Clare wishes to escape from that form of racial imprisonment by bluffing as to her true identity. Yet, to play this role lightly is not easy. Due to the prejudices caused by intolerance of a form of reason too ideological to allow for the needs of individuals, especially a woman, Clare is forced to constantly take precautions against being uncovered by her husband and, in some cases, even by members of her race, who would mark her as a traitor. Her passing must be carefully preserved. It is something mysterious, secret, and attractive, always in danger of being discovered by scrutinizing eyes that have been trained to detect it.

Significantly, a case of passing is the motif of the thriller *Devil in a Blue Dress.* The African American actor Denzel Washington plays a detective in postwar Los Angeles, riven by racial tensions. His role is to untangle an intricate story of love, hate, and greed, centered around a forbidden passion between a white man and a black woman who passes as white. The attraction and admiration of the detective for the latter are not altered in the least by the final discovery that "she passes." The movie was shot in a more tolerant period than the one in which the story is set. There is greater acceptance and understanding toward the positive side of passing than there was in the period when Larsen wrote her novel. The woman who passes, played by Jennifer Beals, is not simply destined by the author to a tragic end but, in fact, is the one who eventually saves the detective's life. She shares certain traits with Clare: she is ambivalent, complex, tormented, reticent, and fascinating, but she does not have the same *maudit* aura of Larsen's heroine. From the start, we have the disquieting feeling that a tragic end awaits Clare. Already from the first chance meeting with Irene, which perturbs Clare, we realize that she has embarked on an irreversible process that will take her back to her roots and to her doom. Her recurring guilt feelings for having *betrayed* her memories are coupled with her obsessive need to be with her people, to "hear them laugh and talk"; she regrets her flight and wishes to go back. But it is too late to go back. From Clare's initial emotional state and from the emphasis placed on the hypothetical "if things had gone differently," it is quite obvious that the journey to the past is a one-way ride. The return to her origins, rather than leading Clare, as biblical-cathartic rhetoric might suggest, to her redemption, leads her to her doom, precisely because in "redeeming" her, it returns her to that which is familiar and friendly. It is as if the curiosity for Clare's passing—characterizing both Irene, who functions as Clare's mirror image, and, indirectly, the author—were ultimately responsible for Clare's destiny. From the start of the story we find a pervasive guilt feeling, the fear that being interested in a different point of view and attributing to it any kind of value is equivalent to betraying one's belonging. At the same time, there is a fascination with Clare's passing and the indirect admission that once the boundaries of belonging have been crossed, there is no turning back. The disapproval Irene feels for Clare's behavior, as soon as she discovers what she is up to, coupled with the curiosity that prevents her from leaving, as she intended to, are symptoms of the ambivalent feelings of the author.

> The waiter returned with Clare's change. Irene reminded herself that she ought immediately to go. But she didn't move.
>
> The truth was, she was curious. There were things she wanted to ask Clare Kendry. She wished to find out about this hazardous business of "passing," this breaking away from all that was familiar and friendly to take one's chance *in another environment, not entirely strange, perhaps, but certainly not entirely friendly.* What, for example, one did about background, how one accounted for oneself. And how one felt when one came into contact with other Negroes. But she couldn't. She was unable to think of a single question that in its context or its phrasing was not too frankly curious, if not actually impertinent.[5]

To make up for this interest, the final punishment administered against the culprit is absolute. Yet, notwithstanding her personal ambition and obstinacy, Clare does not emerge in the end as a negative character, though her self-centeredness and selfishness are frequently brought out. She constantly takes risks and constantly undermines the certainties and beliefs on which her friend has based her whole life. She does not lie to her friend, nor does she wish to repress her affections or erase her original ties, of which she misses the sense of familiarity. The author acknowledges this on various occasions. In fact, the author's choice to have her experience her alterity as a fault and to remember her past with nostalgia, while giving the whole tale a moralistic cast, also expresses the awareness that once we venture beyond the boundaries of the known, like Ulysses at Hercules' pillars, there is no turning back.

From the start, Irene is fascinated by her friend, even though she despises her for having rejected the natural foundation of racial division. She is fond of her despite her disapproval and feels the racial tie as something to protect, a duty she is bound by, more than a desire. But her fate in the end is no better than that of her friend: "[Irene] couldn't betray Clare, couldn't even run the risk of appearing to defend a people that were being maligned, for fear that that defence might in some infinitesimal degree lead the way to final discovery of her secret. She had to Clare Kendry a duty. She was bound to her by those very ties of race, which, for all her repudiation of them, Clare had been unable to completely sever.[6]

Irene is especially interested in Clare's choice and is curious to know what it means to live life day by day when one is passing. She is shocked by her friend's behavior, yet she thinks and talks about it during the entire story. Clare continues to meet with Irene in spite of her friend's efforts to avoid her. The plot gets more complicated when Clare moves for a time to New York and, unknown to her husband, starts visiting Harlem. Her charm and elegance are irresistible to Irene's friends, including Irene's husband, but Clare hides her terrible secret from everyone except Irene. "She is sleeping with the enemy"; she has betrayed her race and origins; she hides, she lies, she lives with a man who hates blacks. Territories are defined, staked, and cannot be changed. Intelligence with the enemy is not permitted. The historical period does not allow it: the harshness and intolerance of racial divisions in the years of segregation leave no room. The suspense increases; Clare's game becomes riskier and riskier, but she cannot stop or change course. It is as if the author herself were cruelly leading her protagonist step by step to the tragic end, when, after her husband discovers her at a party of black people in Harlem, Clare commits suicide. One gets the impression that the death of the heroine is due to the author's need to punish herself for the attraction she shows, page after page, for the practice of passing. Clare is unquestionably the main character in the story. Irene is only an alter ego, serving as a counterpoint to Clare's vitality, freedom, independence, and autonomy. Certainly, she is no less selfish than her friend is. She represses her deepest desires and mechanically follows her sense of racial duty. This is due to conformism more than a sense of pride in her race, something that would have allowed her to understand the injustice of segregation. Irene is not proud of being black. Later on we understand that she rejects passing not because she sees it as a form of betrayal, but only because she is afraid of going beyond the boundaries of racial binarism that passing undermines. She leads a boring life entirely within the conventions of the lower-middle class. Her marriage is shaky; she has given up any possibility for self-realization; her belonging is already established and clearly outlined. Change, risk, and novelty frighten her. Her whole life has been based on security, normality, and the humdrum of everyday existence. The experience of passing, which constantly challenges every aspect of one's life, is too risky for her. Irene seems to sense that passing would bring new possibilities, reveal new perspectives, but this is precisely what she fears.

The story is about a condemnation of passing, yet, at the same time, it represents an effort to justify it. Not on the basis of banal, practical arguments ("our society is racist and everyone must do what he or she can to survive"), which in fact are negatively viewed, but because of the alternative possibilities it offers—for example, that of being visible without being actually seen. In the novel we find a mixture of moralism and racial pride, along with constant comments that denote an interest in this perspective. Visibility is a leitmotif of the entire story and extends from the mysterious fascination exerted by those who practice it to the restless curiosity of those who observe it and speak of it. Passing, as Irene tells a friend, endows one with a power that is denied to white people; it is a one-way experience, practiced only by blacks, which allows one to experience both sides of racial affiliation and therefore neither one. The comment of Irene's husband is illuminating. Irene, who is in fact white enough to pass, meets Clare's racist husband, who does not know he is in the presence of a black who can pass. In response to his declared hatred of blacks, Irene's husband illustrates for her all that passing can offer: "you, my dear, had all the advantage. You knew what his opinion of you was, while he [. . .] We know, always have. They don't. Not quite. It has, you will admit, a humorous side, and, sometimes, its conveniences.[7]

Passing is a subversive form of counter-power, unseen and invisible. Through it blacks undermine white culture because they prevent it from achieving a complete understanding of their alterity. At the same time they participate in it, altering its traits and purity. The impossibility of being totally read, the allure of ambiguity, the possibility of playing on different levels, are recurring themes in the text. The most interesting and most complex character in the novel is Clare, as we have seen, who can be interpreted from various perspectives, like the text as a whole, on account of her ability to play different roles and move in different directions. She is the traitor, the femme fatale, but also the one who is able to escape univocal interpretations, the freest and most autonomous among the characters. If we were to adopt a cyber narrative strategy, we could say that Clare, by teaching the power of the margins and disassembling the concept of racial identity, questions the project of a common language and falsifies the original myth of belonging. Notwithstanding her feelings and her desire to return to her roots, which betray her and are ultimately the cause of her death, Clare is able to undermine the absolute authority of the enemy's culture, because she plays with it. She is certainly the most compromised subject, but she is also the one who is able to understand and fully experience the complexity and multidimensionality of the reality she is immersed in. She plays with differences. Borders become less rigid, fuzzier. Belonging is no longer clear-cut. Even Irene, notwithstanding her disapproval of passing, is surprised by the attention it attracts and asks herself to what it may be due. "It's funny about 'passing.' We disapprove of it and at the same time condone it. It excites our contempt and yet we rather admire it. We shy away from it with an odd kind of revulsion, but we protect it."[8]

Passing is a form of ambiguity that must be protected. Its subversiveness lies precisely in the possibility of entering unknown territory, "not entirely strange . . . not entirely friendly." Passing is "Intelligence with the enemy," an erotic surrender to the other, who is ultimately, as in this case, a part of ourselves. From the start, Irene has rejected this option, though she is aware that she is white enough to pass. Emotionally, she moves in a twilight zone, caught between the fear of breaking boundaries and an unconscious desire to be free. She knows that this is part of *her self* and of the process through which that self is constructed, i.e., of the inner and outer image of *her self* in relation to the other. But she is also afraid of this and of possible consequences. She is afraid of her deepest and most unconscious desires. The possibility of investigating her self is set aside in favor of the reassuring phantasm of "difference," which projects its protective shadow and weakens any effort to break the boundaries of belonging. The difference (being black) is perceived as diversity from that which is the same (being white) and creates belonging mechanisms that defend what is certain, what is defined as different. Difference is perceived as a reassuring place, which eliminates all tensions and contrasts. Irene's husband would like to move out of Harlem, but Irene tells him she would rather stay where she feels safe. And she does not even want to discuss the problem of racial discrimination with her sons. They will learn later on their own. Stability and the narrow-mindedness of petit-bourgeois values are what shield her from the danger of novelty. Confronted with the external world where contradictions explode and "blacks are lynched," but where there is also the possibility of fighting, of liberating desire, Irene takes refuge in difference, which she turns into the safe niche of subalternity. *Safe* is a word that Irene constantly repeats, succeeding in transforming her difference into indifference. On safety she has based her whole existence. But safety is also what causes her dissatisfaction. Being black is a given that she does not reject. It is a given. But at the same time, she is aware that it oppresses and stifles her. It imposes on her a loyalty that she is afraid to reject, but would like to avoid in the name of an unknown, mysterious desire buried deep inside her. Racial belonging defines her difference as something that denies her other experiences, the experience of passing for example. For Irene, this is not solely a racial issue, which, as she understands, can sometimes be willingly chosen, but something that has to do with the most intimate part of her being. "Race! The thing that bound and suffocated her [. . .] Sitting alone in the quiet living-room in the pleasant fire light, Irene Redfield wished, for the first time in her life, that she had not been born a Negro. For the first time she suffered and rebelled because she was unable to disregard the burden of race. It was, she cried silently, enough to suffer as a woman, an individual, on one's own account, without having to suffer for the race as well. It was a brutality, and undeserved. Surely, no other people so cursed as Ham's dark children."[9]

But precisely because she is a woman, she is allowed to glimpse for an instant a different view of the concept of difference, connected to her body and its materiality. Irene—who up to now has reacted to Clare's double betrayal (after having betrayed her origins, Clare has also betrayed their friendship by stealing Irene's husband) by remaining attached to protecting her privileges—now feels the oppression of belonging, while at the same time she understands the meaning of discrimination for the first time. Therefore, she begins to question all her certainties: belonging, marriage, love. She asks herself whether she might not desire something more than a calm, routine life. She realizes she does. But, for her, it is easier to preserve what she has rather than experiment with novelty. Clare represents everything that undermines her world. Even her husband has fallen in love with Clare's independence, though he believes in the pride of racial belonging and the opposition against segregation, which is certainly not served by passing. Then why? Perhaps it is the fascination with the unknown, the different, the new. Just what Irene fears and wishes to avoid. Thus, her self-questioning does not last for long. She immediately falls back on the stereotypes that make her feel protected and safe.

Irene understands that her sexual difference, her being a woman, exposes her to suffering and humiliation. In front of a Lacanian mirror she speaks to her image, understands the power of desire, but is unable to overcome the temptation to give up. For a moment she clearly perceives her condition, yet she chooses her shackles. For the first time she understands her deepest self, but she is unable to surrender herself to it, to turn it into an instrument of power to free her from the ties that imprison her. Precisely her condition as woman, which at first allows her to perceive her subaltern position and that of her race, becomes the justification of this subalternity. Hers is a gilded cage. Irene understands the slavery of belonging, of origins, but she chooses to sink back into them, to allow them to suffocate her, in parallel with Clare, who commits suicide.

> Was it, perhaps, that she had endured all that a woman could endure of tormenting humiliation and fear? Or was it that she lacked the capacity for the acme of suffering? [. . .] Security. Was it just a word? If not, then was it only by the sacrifice of other things, happiness, love, or some wild ecstasy that she had never known, that it could be obtained? And did too much striving, too much faith in safety and permanence, unfit one for these other things?
>
> Irene didn't know, couldn't decide, though for a long time she sat questioning and trying to understand. Yet all the while, in spite of her searchings and feeling of frustration, she was aware that, to her, security was the most important and desired thing in life. Not for any of the others, or for all of them, would she exchange it. She wanted only to be tranquil . . .
>
> [She] could think again of ways to keep Brian by her side, and in New York. For she would not go to Brazil. She belonged to this land of rising towers. She was an American. She grew from this soil, and she would not be uprooted. [. . .]
>
> Brian, too, belonged here. His duty was to her and to his boys.
>
> Strange, that she couldn't now be sure that she had ever truly known love. Not even for Brian. He was her husband and the father of her sons. But was he anything more? Had she ever wanted or tried for more? In that hour she thought not.
>
> Nevertheless, she meant to keep him. Her freshly painted lips narrowed to a thin straight line. . . . She still intended to hold fast to the outer shell of her marriage, to keep her life fixed, certain. Brought to the edge of a distasteful reality, her fastidious nature did not recoil.[10]

Clare represents an escape from the limitation of what is known and defined, but her past frightens and haunts her. In spite of this, through Irene, she returns to it, because it is ultimately reassuring. Her need for reassurance, her self-centeredness, and her feelings of guilt cause her to engage in a dangerous game. In Irene's case, instead, the fear of fragmentation, a *horror vacui,* activate reaggregation processes that hinder possible transformations of the self. Racial difference is perceived as a reassuring place where contrasts and tensions are absent. Irene is condemned to a lack of desire that stifles and finally quenches the most vital part of her being. The two women, who in their parallel paths are always shifting between inner contradictions and discontinuities, highlight the beauty and danger of the process of disidentification. Along with the loneliness that the absence of reference points may cause, which can lead to mental alienation, there is the joyous risk of choosing various perspectives of observation and action. Both women glimpse the possibility of choosing paths that would expose them to the external world, but the need for security stops them. They choose to betray their *selves,* rather than give in to the beauty of the fluidity of desire, the beauty of being nomadic, as we would say today. Larsen's emphasis, notwithstanding the condemnation based on the ideology of racial betrayal, seems to me fundamentally directed toward the fascination, forbidden at the time, of what we may define as a free fluctuation of identity, a process in which she sees danger, but also the subversive and liberating potential. This is the beauty and the danger of deconstructing the self: *disidentification.* Throughout the novel, in spite of her moralistic stance, Larsen condemns the selfishness of both women, their betrayal of themselves. The one is the victim of her regrets and her guilt feelings; the other chooses the sterile certainties of stability over her internal freedom. Unfaithfulness to any belonging can be addictive to the point of self-destruction, but it is also the harbinger of new horizons—so the writer seems to say. Having intuited the disruptive power of passing, she lets us indirectly perceive its positive side.

It is significant that this novel, anticipating themes that are especially relevant today, is dominated by a female presence that is very contradictory but, at the same time, very intense, and certainly more important than the male presence. The two female characters take up practically the entire novel. Men are mostly absent, and when they do appear on stage, they are not particularly interesting. In fact, they serve as a prop for women, seldom speaking except to answer female characters. In these monologue-dialogues, it is the female voice that speaks, expressing the importance of escaping the domain of belonging. This subjectivity was one that had always been used for evasion and withdrawal to the shadows of internal spaces and affections. Frequently, the two main characters speak of the limitations imposed on them by their social role within their families and within their relation with their partner, even though their relative well being serves to alleviate some of the responsibilities of a patriarchal and bourgeois society. Nevertheless, there are well-defined, specific rules that relegate them to a marginal world. Forms of asymmetry between the male and female roles are suggested in a more or less direct way. Guilt feelings, responsibilities, social and sexual roles, all these curtail the range of their choices and are frequently the subject of their discussions. This brings about a degree of complicity between the two women, who share secrets that are unknown to their partners, independently of racial differences. An extended network of relations and power juxtapositions is created. Larsen perceives the radicalness to which passing can lead, breaking the oppressive shackles of original ties. Certainly, the author is forced by the pressure of her period to choose the safe and proud haven of belonging and memory and to punish Clare's betrayal with death and Irene's conformity with "social" death. But we could also turn this argument around, maintaining that the author condemns the two characters because they lack the courage to let the desire for a new construction of the self prevail over the safety of belonging.

I read this novel with the awareness that the navigation in uncharted and sometimes hostile waters is now free of the encumbrance of ideologies. I have borrowed my title from it, with the joyous realization that there are no betrayals to condemn or safe harbors to repair to, even for one night, but that, on the contrary, there is only a form of mobility, where the journey is more important than the destination. Although there may be maps showing the best routes or providing information on the sea floor, the realization is now generally accepted that navigation is a process; it is similar to what takes place when we shift from the surface of the sea to the mental surface of communication between human beings and machines. This realization has guided me in the present narrative journey. In particular, insofar as the development of mechanical intelligence and the modern liberation of women are contemporary in patriarchal history, as Sadie Plant reminds us, I wish to emphasize that the fact that they both function according to a process of simulation is due to the absence of clearly defined identities. For this reason they are susceptible to unpredictable future developments. The disadvantage of coming from a history of exclusion is transformed into an advantage that, by appropriating the technology of the present transitional period, helps further the process of redefining identity. The fact of being absent, hidden, invisible, which was part of the female handicap, is transformed, in the digital era, from a handicap into the possibility of attaining an unprecedented agility and lightness. Women occupy a privileged position within a journey, in which the goal is to become cybernauts of the collective mind, navigating techno-mediatic flows of network information, where individuals are terminal identities. In these circumstances there are many maps, sometimes contradictory, and routes can lead to unforeseen destinations. It is in this context and with this attitude that I wish to analyze, in the next chapter, the functional mechanisms of memory in human beings and machines, comparing their characteristics and examining their interactions, for the purpose of demonstrating that there are multiple ways for us to react to the epochal mutation we are undergoing and to the disorientation it generates. We can choose the safe harbor of reterritorialization, on the roots of our belonging and of the memory that gives purity. But we can also open ourselves to the deterritorialization that technology produces. The machine can serve to indicate the modalities for reconfiguring concepts, helping to uproot mental constructions that previous models had created. The obsession with the original myth and the concept of identity, tied to a social and political universe that is pathetically falling apart, causes the system to react aggressively to planetary contamination, determined to assert a nostalgic territorialization, the mummification of memory. Women are the first victims of this nostalgia, since the return to the past almost always entails the reinstatement of models that tend to negate the achievements of female and feminist movements. This regression is opposed by the project of nomadism, which, in contrast, is realized through participation in variable, provisional, communitarian paradigms, such as those created in the unstable encounters of the Internet.

Rerun the Memory

AMNESIA, AT LEAST FROM A CLINICAL PERSPECTIVE, IS A DISORDER THAT affects memory. Two types of amnesia are particularly common: the first is caused by psychological shock, the second is due to physiological pathologies. Asthma, encephalitis, and paralysis are among the causes of the latter and more serious form of amnesia.

In the first case, it is possible, using medical or psychoanalytical techniques, to recover the past, bypassing the defense mechanism that prevents memory from being accessed. One can be normal again. We all remember Hitchcock's *Spellbound,* in which Gregory Peck is a patient who cannot recall certain areas of his past experience; he is disturbed by images that trigger unwelcome memories but in the end is finally cured through the tender care of psychoanalyst Ingrid Bergman.

In the second case, however, brain cells are irreparably damaged, burned out, and cannot be replaced. There are no triggers that can help recover the lost past. The result is that those who suffer from this type of amnesia remember almost nothing of the remote past and little of the more recent past. They live almost entirely in the present and in a state of almost complete isolation.

Strangely enough, these patients, except for occasional moments of insecurity, are usually quite tranquil, free of the nervous and depressive states common after a certain age. But, they are not self-sufficient and are incapable of organizing their lives. They need someone constantly at their side, because they cannot perform even the simplest everyday activities, since even these are dependent on memory. They are incapable of remembering they should do something or that they have just done it. A seriously ill patient can tell the same anecdote twenty-five times in an hour, without remembering ever having told it. It is a sort of mental incontinence. The mysterious connotations of this mental disorder and the state of vulnerability of the victim of amnesia have often inspired the fantasy of writers and movie makers. In these stories, shady characters seek to exploit the situation to their advantage or even to directly induce states of amnesia in the mind of their victim for their own dark purposes. For memory is a strange faculty. It can be very sharp and reliable, recalling the most trivial details of past events; at the same time, its actual functioning is still largely unknown, and its vulnerability to tricks and errors limits its reliability. Memories, scientifically speaking, are not the equivalent of photos or texts, stored inside the brain where they lie unaltered until recalled. The configuration of the memory is periodically modified, and the same event is remembered and narrated differently at different moments. The biologist Gerald Edelman argues that when we memorize information, this influences the information already stored in memory, restructuring its representation, and in turn is influenced by the "circularity" of individual events that have been experienced and memorized. There is a continuous comparison between immediate experience, present memories, and future expectations, an incessant activity that goes back and forth, updating old memory configurations and reelaborating new information. Individual memory is therefore mutable and, being related to emotions, is a far cry from an objective, permanent record of an event. Memory, by its very nature, is cross-eyed.

Certainly memory needs an external stimulus, or trigger, to call up the past and its associated emotions. Proust's *Madeleine* is the most famous literary example. Memory is a fundamental element in the construction of individual identity, and when it is pathologically altered like amnesia, it creates in the individual a serious form of mental aging. The moment the mentally ill individual stops to tell his/her story, it becomes his/her entire life's span. It becomes all he/she can remember of his/her entire lifetime in its flowing, at least for the short space he/she is able to preserve its memory. It is easy to grasp how readily people who suffer from amnesia can be fooled and are completely dependent on other people's memory. It is a horrendous crime to exploit a mentally ill person. When the victim is healthy, the criminal's tactic is to convince the institutional authorities that he/she is incapable of independent judgment, is mentally degenerating, and must be constantly supervised and directed. Self-sufficiency, strictly dependent on the capacity to remember, must be undermined. *Triggers* are artificially created to induce the victim to remember, after which the deceiver convinces him or her that that past never existed. Doubt insinuates itself in the mind of the designated targets who, if their memory is constantly challenged and the deception is well organized, start doubting their sanity. This is what happens in *Gas Light,* directed by George Cukor in 1946, as a remake of a 1939 British film, based in turn on a novel by Patrick Hamilton. In the movie, an evil governess, Angela Lansbury, and a cold and cruel husband, Charles Boyer, conspire to undermine the sanity of the victim, Ingrid Bergman, stealing her memory, all for a handful of jewels.

Memory can thus be easily undermined when one lacks external evidence in support of one's recollections or when these are not shared by other people. Individuals become *disoriented* and confused and the external world seems to escape their grasp. The trigger brings back memories, activating feelings and desires to which memory is always connected, and establishing a connection with the unconscious and its complex, mysterious processes. Insofar as it is connected to each person's individual experience, memory lacks any objectivity and is a matter of personal feeling, a feeling inextricably interfaced with the construction of personal identity and with the way other people perceive it.

In the movie *The Net,* the protagonist Angela Bennet (Sandra Bullock) is a computer expert. She repairs the damage to computer memory caused by viruses or errors. When she accidentally receives a disk that was not meant for her, she runs into trouble to the point of losing her past and her identity. Angela is well-known to the Internet virtual community, but as a physical person she does not exist. She does not even have a name. Someone else takes her place and when she comes back from a vacation in Mexico, her past has been erased. Her memory is obliterated by an external agent, like a computer attacked by a virus. Like a reset computer, Angela finds another name and a new past. She is in a muddle, but her computer expertise helps her. She decides to react against the external agent that has destroyed her memory (a group of conspirators, extravagantly named "The Praetorians," who seek to seize power through computers). Using her technical skills and the help, at least in an early phase, of a young psychoanalyst who believes her story, she counterattacks. Like the androids in *Blade Runner,* she tries to escape beyond the control of those who direct her existence. This time it is a human being who is dominated by machines, though these are ultimately directed by people. More like a female version of Indiana Jones than a nerdy hacker, she starts tracking down the conspirators. Quick and precise like a cyborg in identifying her targets, Angela gradually reconstructs the steps through which her social memory has been erased and finds the culprits. It is interesting to note how the protagonist achieves her goal using her flexibility and lightness as a weapon against her adversaries. Angela is in a paradoxical situation: despite the material presence of her body, she has been denied an identity and therefore existence. She counteracts this by adopting a physical and psychological mobility very similar to what is used in the Internet cyberspace. She uses whatever computers she comes across, manipulating the machines to unmask the criminals. With the same nonchalance and circumspection with which she sat down to work at the computer, she abandons it, knowing that while it is unlikely that she will ever sit down there again, one's material location is irrelevant in cyberspace.

There are two interesting novelties in this movie. The first is that it is no longer necessary to be a man in order to play the main role in a movie with a sophisticated technological background. Force and violence are no longer essential because agility and lightness are more effective. It is significant that the liberal director, Irwin Winkler, who in 1991 directed a movie on the McCarthy era, should choose a woman to tell this story. Notwithstanding the brutal erasure of her identity, Angela does not lose heart and moves self-confidently in no-man's land, conscious of her inclination for invisibility and anonymity.

The second characteristic is the analogy between the protagonist's profession and the frontal attack against her memory and identity. Angela, who cures computers from their cerebral concussions, giving them back their memory, has her own memory erased from the outside; thus, a parallel is established between sentient and mechanical organisms. This parallel is certainly no novelty in modern scientific thought, but it is particularly relevant in the present period, when we are experiencing an uncontrolled proliferation of infosphericsignals, produced by media communication sources, which constantly beset the human mind. This parallel leads to important reflections on the subjectivity of identity processes, whose construction is based, among other components, on the ability of historic and individual memories to retain information. We are undergoing a period of unprecedented technological expansion, and the interweaving of organic and mechanical elements is causing a mutation that forces us to reconsider the meaning and function of memory. It has been said that we are moving from the Neolithic age to the Noolithic, that is an era of the predominance of the mind (*noos* in Greek means mind). There is an asymmetry between the unlimited proliferation of information signals and their interaction with the world of events (infosphere), and the capacity of human beings to assimilate information. This asymmetry causes at the same time disorientation and a search for new horizons and uncontrolled spaces. The infospheric connections create an unlimited series of contacts between humans and machines, which resemble the contacts of nerve cells in the human brain (synapses). A great social brain is produced, what Pierre Lévy calls the *collective intelligence,* and this forces us to reconsider the social attitudes of individuals and in general the relationship with Otherness. In this new anthropological space of knowledge, where otherness is viewed positively, social ties are subject to an engineering process that, by interfacing individual human and machine intelligence, gives rise to virtual communities where no form of mediation is necessary. Individual and collective memories lose their centrality as the stable witness of historic development, which implodes upon contact with the machine world. The incessant explosion of information signals produces an inflation of meaning which anesthetizes the capability to absorb them by thinking organisms, and memory becomes incontinent. The infinite possibilities of this anthropological mutation generate an information magma that disorients human beings. Bifo writes: "Neuromagma is the chaos-motic vortex in which the late-modern sentient organism is caught and where all sense of direction is lost. But it is also the vortex where new receptive-projective configurations of the organism develop, which are new modes of neurological interaction."[1]

We are "input and output terminals" of this vortex, whose crucial elements are the technological mutation we are experiencing and the capacity of interconnected human minds to absorb the enormous mass of information arriving from the infosphere. These processes of deterritorialization developing in technological capitalism are associated with processes of identity reterritorialization, which seek to respond to the disorientation and the need for acknowledgment, tending to fall back on the myth of origins as an answer to computer metastasis. This is precisely what makes a close comparison between humans and machines necessary.

The contradictory and fascinating relation between the human mind and the machine has been already discussed by Norbert Wiener, the theoretical father of computer technology, who in 1948 wrote *Cybernetics: or Control and Communication in the Animal and the Machine.* In the chapter "Computing Machines and the Nervous System," Wiener compares the animal nervous system to computing machines. Neurons receive and transmit messages from and to other neurons through contacts called synapses, which vary in number from one neuron to the other and serve to activate the functioning of neurons, which are also "excited" by other functions, not necessarily neuronic, like those of a "humoral nature." In the adult human brain there are one hundred trillion such contacts. Wiener compares them to the internal relays in computers in order to describe their ability to memorize, that is, "the ability to preserve the results of past operations for use in the future."[2] Wiener's idea is that the similarities and differences evidenced by the comparison between the functioning of computing machines and that of the brain may be useful in the disciplines of psychopathology and psychiatry in the cure of nervous system disorders, aside from its obvious interest for the branch of mathematics that studies communication. The word *cybernetics,* in fact, comes from the Greek *kybernetiké,* "the art of piloting," and is the discipline that studies "the field of control and communication theory whether in the machine or in the animal."[3] This was a science that began to develop before World War II and was initially stimulated by the need to create a fast and efficient air force to use against Nazi Germany. Military needs and the start of the war had a decisive influence on the development of this "male" and patriarchal science, having power and domination as its goals. In peacetime, however, Wiener and other scientists were joined by a number of intellectuals, such as Gregory Bateson and Margaret Mead, who certainly could not be accused of warlike or militarist attitudes. Initially, the project focused on the improvement of security systems, organized as a system going from the human brain to machines and back again. At its core were processes of communication and memory. The programming of the machine focused on what the male human mind sought to penetrate, though we should remember that one of the first computer programmers was a woman, Ada Lovelace.

Wiener mentions two types of memory in relation to both the human mind and machines. The first is the short term memory, which immediately stores information and can be both read and erased very rapidly. This serves to perform operations such as multiplication, whose intermediate results are of no interest and in which the operating apparatus is later freed for further communicative purposes. In the human brain, this memory is based on a sequence of impulses that travel in a closed circuit until they are erased from the outside. This mechanism can be easily reproduced by various computing devices.

The other type is the long-term memory, which, in both human brain and machine, stores the entire "document" or file, creating a permanent memory, and contributes to future behavior at least for a single "run" in the case of the machine and for the entire lifetime of a human being. The machine can be reprogrammed many times and thus be used for several "runs," whereas the human brain cannot. As psychoanalysis has shown, the human brain never stops functioning even when we "disconnect" from the external world in order to sleep. Notwithstanding the similarity between their mechanism for storing information, there is a fundamental difference between humans and machines. It consists in the fact that: "The machine is intended for many successive runs without reference to each other . . . and it can be cleared between such runs while the brain under normal circumstances is not the complete analogue of the computing machine, but rather the analogue of a single run."[4]

According to Wiener, there are two necessary conditions for reproducing the capabilities of human memory in a machine: the first is that the impulse be transmitted through a medium capable of achieving an acceptable time-lag; the second is that this impulse be reconstructed with extreme precision. But the fundamental requirement is that the transmission be activated by a trigger, as in the human brain. The brain, as recent studies have shown, creates a multidimensional model of experience—akin to what in current computer terminology would be called a windows system—which can be easily recalled. The more a given synaptic path is followed, the easier it is to trigger that specific memory. The system, called *windows opportunity for learning,* reaches the apex of its activity at the age of ten-twelve, though, as we know, individuals continue learning throughout their lives. In his recent *A Celebration of Neurons,* Robert Sylvester states that knowledge is more easily retained by elementary school children (between six and 12) if information is not simply transmitted in oral form and stored in memory exclusively as an aural stimulus, but rather is associated to tactile and emotional ones. Sylvester suggests that good teachers, aside from explaining and illustrating material orally, create situations in which children can actively participate in the story that is being told. For example, in history, if they wish to speak of the Civil War, they could involve youngsters in the dramatization of the event of a famous battle, having them act it out, thus becoming part of the historical event. One should set aside notebooks for a while, says Sylvester, and start building a model battlefield. In this activity, all the senses must be involved: smell (glue used to position soldiers on the flat surface of the paper); sight (the strategic disposition of the soldiers on the battlefield); and touch (used in creating the battlefield and manipulating the soldiers). Through this technique, the main episodes of the battle can be memorized in the form of a multidimensional mental model, which can be more easily recalled when necessary. These assumptions could revolutionize our teaching system, for which memorization is based mainly on oral and written transmission.

As Wiener shows, in the electrical industry, the capacity to recall memories was initially stimulated in connection with telegraph circuits capable of producing effects similar to mnemonic triggers, though the impossibility of developing the equivalent of a long-term memory was initially an obstacle, later overcome.

The problem of storing information is due to changes in the neuron threshold or, more specifically, changes in the permeability of each synapse in relation to specific messages. This happens through the opening of new paths and the closing of old ones. Since not only are no new neurons created after birth, but sometimes not even new synapses, it is conceivable that the greatest changes in threshold levels of the memorization process are only increases in its capacity. The human brain is already "wired" at birth and has built-in time limits. These are called "critical periods;" these limits are represented by those "windows" that nature opens at our birth and shuts down one after the other as our birthdays gently roll by. A maximum in learning capability, connected to the self-conscious articulation of knowledge, is reached around the age of twelve. As Wiener comments: "Our whole life is on the pattern of Balzac's Peau de Chagrin and the very process of learning and remembering exhausts our powers of learning and remembering until life itself squanders our capital stock of power to live."[5]

The ability to learn and to memorize by enlarging our memory shrinks itself, shrinking our power to remember as well as our lives, like the skin donated to Raphael in Balzac's novel. The normal process of senility, which is compounded by other complex factors, becomes pathological when nerve cells become completely incapable of retention. In amnesia, for example, neurons are destroyed, memory falters, and mental disorders develop. The same thing happens in a computer when it crashes and all the data on its hard drive is erased. But while the brain has only one run at its disposal, the computer is programmed to perform multiple runs at incredible speed.

In the present age, the enormous mass of information arriving from the infosphere saturates the human brain, which becomes incapable of absorbing and memorizing it, thus risking impotence and destruction. The machine-originated deconstruction of the human mind and human memory—which is a fundamental component of personality—along with the destructuring of the individual ego from past encrustations, certainly comes dangerously close to the infinite permeability of information flows, but at the same time gives us the liberty to express feelings, pain, and desire through the medium of those flows. It is essential to prepare individual and collective memories for the possibility of adopting various individual paths, like the machine—"multiple runs," to use Wiener's expression. To restructure memory processes, to rerun the memory, exploiting the fact that memory is never a photographic reproduction of reality and that, therefore, it is possible to rewrite the past, destroying the purity of events, the historical objectivity of its development and of the associated symbolical system is to rewrite the present.

This path is particularly suited to women, for they have been traditionally deprived of memory and of the possibility to bear witness. As Lea Melandri writes, we share ". . . the sad privilege of one who suffers from amnesia, who will never know whether he/she is reconstructing his/her life or encountering his/her birth for the first time."[6] Through the *escamotage* of the machine, I see the possibility of evading cultural models that have imposed the imitation of man on us women as the precondition for our entrance into a domain that did not belong to us, where a strong, compact identity was an essential advantage, the only one that entitled one to visibility and, therefore, to memory. To this we bear witness. Today there is no longer any need for that identity, and the more memory, the foundation of the formation of identity, shows the signs of historical temporality, the closer we get to the disappearance of the model of reason it represents and from which it is only apparently separated. In *The Picture of Dorian Gray,* through a diabolical pact, the portrait ages while the body maintains its youth. In the same way, historical memory is only apparently separated from the materiality of a rationality of which man is the only visible bearer, but in fact it gives eternity to the male body, which comprises language, knowledge, and the identity that it represents. When the mutation we are undergoing rends the veil of memory, which, coagulated in the wounds of time, has been accumulated by that identity throughout a history constructed as the mirror of its omnipotence, it irreversibly destroys its existence, revealing the material bias on which the universal pretensions of its subjectivity had been constructed. The emperor has no clothes. The irony lies in the fact that this mutation takes place thanks to a science of patriarchal origin. The technological products generated by it are the legitimate offspring, which, independent of current efforts to regulate it, are open to new presences. The paradox is that the machine created in the image of men can become the instrument suited to the expression of women's affections, feelings, and dreams. From a survey published by *Newsweek* in 1994, we learn that while the attraction of the machine, for men, lies in its extension of physical power, for women it lies in the capacity to satisfy needs and desires. Also, women prefer working in groups rather than alone, are attracted to nonlinear games, i.e., games having more than one solution, and they do not like to see the protagonists of those video games die. The number of women who work as computer experts and who access Internet sites is expected to rise constantly at least in the next ten years. A great step forward, considering the militarist origin of computer science, born out of the violence of a theoretical framework in response to military needs. Certainly, there is a risk of disorientation, yet, for the time being at least, it is more than offset by the advantage of the radical adventure of navigating without goals. The capacity for disidentification necessary to reprogram the memory in this way is more available to women, traditionally deprived of a strong identity. This does not require us to forget the past that excluded us and the present that is still characterized by a strong asymmetry between men and women. Nor are we required to give up the idea of constructing a different type of memory, which may represent our presence and transmit it to the future.

It is important, however, that this presence not be crystallized or mummified in forms of representative mediations having universal pretensions, because this would be nothing but the replication of the tragic error of male history. On the contrary, that past must be turned into an advantage, a place of time-lag, the same time-lag necessary to the sedimentation of memory. The past reveals the delay with which we enter the present stage of history and bears witness to our absence. Thanks to this form of mnemonic fluidity, it never burdens the presence with its weight, like Toni Morrison's ghost, and never lures us into the trap of aspiring to a universal conceptual order. Only in this way can the efforts, struggles, and sufferings of those who have preceded us be remembered. This is the same idea that leads Alain Finkielkraut to state that his being "Jewish" has nothing to do with a sense of belonging to a culture or religion—which, in his case, after the Holocaust, has become a privilege—but with the fact that it renders meaningless the idea of claiming a certain past in order to construct a future based on the limits of that identity.[7] Going beyond the idea of belonging to stable communities with rigid boundaries, such a disposition locates memory in a position that is not instrumental to that which has been or will be. Rather it locates it in a place without foundations, beyond the logic of a social tie generalized indistinctly to all members of that group and only that group. It is advisable for us women to use the memory of our invisibility and marginality, during this period of technological and anthropological mutation, in order to fully experience this transformation, play a major role in it, and influence as much as possible the formation of a new cultural order without establishing specific destinations. In other words, to be light, mobile, and agile, without the weight of resentment or the convenience of a generic belonging, which would belie our past and limit our future. Only in this way can we show our gratitude to the women who have preceded us, preventing them from being forgotten. Thus, the past will not be turned into a dark mirror in which only women are represented, but will rather be a space open to all the subjects who see their image and their history in that symbolic system.

Is there a risk that the shift of interest from man/woman to the machine and the presumed inversion of the process of imitation between humans and machines will lead us on the way to Damascus? Will this convert us to a desire for omnipotence (already experienced throughout the centuries by the male philosophical tradition of Western thought) or, worse, to a new position of subalternity already attacked by the philosophical current of the "theory of difference"? The characteristics of human memory could be transferred to the machine, which would faithfully reproduce them, exploiting its capacity for infinite replication without being bound by physiological limits or a single program, thanks to the various contemporaneous "runs" at its disposal. But what happens when the reverse happens, and the human brain is modeled on the machine? Is this not an effort to transgress the boundaries of what is defined, violating "natural" laws? Is it not a variant of the old ambition, or rather patriarchal obsession, of Western philosophy, namely the desire to play God, represented in a different but no less dangerous form, with the specific goal of achieving a perfection that cannot belong to mankind and that, again, suppresses the mystery of birth being performed through the body of women? The whole of Western philosophy, it can hardly be denied, is centered more on the category of death than on that of life, and, spurred by its drive for omnipotence, has sought to appropriate the process of creation.

The fear of the double is a relatively recent manifestation of that desire, whose most famous literary representation is found in Mary Shelley's *Frankenstein.* Mary Shelley's creation represents an effort to reappropriate a creative process from which she rightly felt excluded. In modern philosophy and science this existential disease, in most cases characteristic of men, has been widely analyzed. From the *Great Turk,* by Baron Von Kempelen, to the recent case of the computer *Deep Blue* that beat capable Kasparov at chess, the figure of the robot has stimulated the fantasy and challenged the creative power of modern human beings during the last two centuries. The most famous movie doubles, from the robot in Fritz Lang's *Metropolis* to the androids, replicas of human beings in Ridley Scott's *Blade Runner,* have fascinated millions of spectators, arousing fear and admiration, even if now we know that, notwithstanding its speed and enormous memory, the computer has problems coping with the surprises and uncertainties associated with the creative behavior of human beings. The fear that machines may run out of control is no longer relegated to science-fiction and will only be overcome if we stop fearing their presence and the fluid energy of our desiring capabilities. Herein lies the novelty. We are no longer dealing with a one-way process by which one imitates the machine and becomes the victim of that process of imitation, thus confirming the neutral characterization elaborated by patriarchal culture. Now the scenario is changing; we move from machine to brain and from brain to machine in a series of interconnections and exploratory journeys where original intentions have lost any capability of matching the actual outcomes. Man and woman no longer wield absolute control over intelligence.

From this perspective, it is my impression that Donna Haraway has already provided us with a number of strategic responses, using the concept of cyborg *t*o redefine the idea of nature itself. Certainly, this poses the problem of the relation between human intelligence and suprahuman or transcendent intelligence, represented by God. Machines are certainly no answer to human beings' irrepressible need for spirituality, which should certainly be discussed much more at length than is possible here. In the context of the machine, this relationship apparently vanishes within the relations among different components of the human mind, which becomes, as suggested by Pierre Lévy, an interface between human and machine, permitting the human agent and the computer system to communicate. That interface establishes a connection between organic and mechanical intelligence and forms the collective intelligence, i.e., the *infinite product* of a human economy, which will never be completely automated.[8] Its materialization leads to the idea, perhaps naive but nevertheless original, of a different type of connection between the technical and social element, through the separation of collective intelligence from the supremacy of economics, a connection that resembles Wiener's "multiple runs." To argue in favor of this change of direction does not mean acritically celebrating technological progress but, on the contrary, being aware that the complex evolution of technology, and of computers in particular, forces us to reconsider certain categories, which have been taken for granted for centuries, in light of the transition we are undergoing. For I am convinced that the only alternative we have is to enter this mutation and to let this mutation enter us.

The problem is not that of optimizing the performance of the human brain, aspiring to a perfection and a control that belong to the male logic of power and domination, but of disassembling the components of the current process of limiting identities that have become ossified and completely unsuitable to the present mutation. In the course of this transformation, presences that the traditional structure of culture and power had made invisible are to be made visible. Felix Guattari speaks of individuals interweaving connections in relation to the association of organic and mechanical components. Such a "rizomatic" process cannot be found in any linguistic or behavioral guide, where the connections of human and machine are open to other combinations. In an infosphere inundated with messages that the sentient organism is incapable of absorbing, cyberspace—through the continually expanding juxtaposition of virtual meeting places in the Internet—increasingly compresses and limits the cybertime humans have at their disposal to elaborate its signals. This creates a state of anxiety, indeed of panic, which manifests itself in forms of reterritorialization based on appeals to belonging, identity, and the memory of origins. That which in pathological terms is an amnesia and, being a physical disorder connected to an emotional one, represents a handicap, in the above situation becomes an advantage. The human mind, incapable of absorbing the savage attacks of the information flood, is faced with a grim choice: territorial reaggregation or the terror of disintegration, cyberfascism, or folly. I believe that a process akin to amnesia, without the loss of the neurons' communicative capabilities, must be taken into consideration, and I propose a sort of *passing* or rather a *rerun* of memory, which must not be erased, cauterized, or even brought back to its original roots in response to a need for security. Instead, we can simply take part in the game of communitarian drift over the Internet, where one can be what one desires and can play without the demon of territoriality, because one lives in the digital dominion of precariousness. Having crossed the boundaries of what is defined, we enter the sphere of virtual reality. But in this process of overcoming the natural laws, where will the sexualized body, which in the case of woman lies at the origin of the creative processes and which has meant and continues to mean so much for contemporary philosophical meditation and the history of women, end up?

Trespassing the Borders

It is no secret that, in the Western philosophical and cultural tradition, the female body, in its materiality, has been appropriated by male predatory reason and language. As the "culture of difference" has shown, those intellectual and physical attributes, belonging to only one of the two genders, were taken to represent the whole. They include the aspiration to objectivity and neutrality that characterizes the dominant form of truth and rationality. The excluded female gender was forced to conform, through a process of imitation, to a totality that presented the male subject and to the form of thought and language used by that subject as if it were universal and neutral. Thus, woman became the other *par excellence,* forced into silence in a context where the word that was denied her was the key to supremacy. The female body, in the course of the various evolutions of a masculine genderized knowledge, is lost; it is absorbed by the primacy of reason, which, being the product of male subjectivity, manifests itself in a specular game of self-reflection.

Foucault, Deleuze, and Guattari, among the modern thinkers who have reflected on the origin of modernity, have the merit of having given unprecedented attention to the body, subjecting it to philosophical analysis and combining it with technical mechanical elements. As the focus of a multiplication of discourses and normalizing knowledge drives, the body has become the subject of scientific knowledge and social consideration. Thus Foucault, interpreting sexuality as the development of a "complex political technology" and the body as a source of power, has returned to it a value that had been impoverished by psychoanalysis and ideology. Redesigning the bodily structure of subjectivity, the male nature of philosophical knowledge is revealed. Deleuze and Guattari, with their schizo-analysis, emphasize the erotic character of the desiring machine that makes the body the central focus of their analysis, albeit with no distinction of gender.

What makes these theoretical formulations interesting from a feminist perspective is the fact that they represent the relationships among individuals as relations of power that lie at the core of the institution of sexuality and the division of social and political roles among the sexes.

Yet those who have truly given back the female body its materiality, exalting its difference from the male body, are, among others, the theoreticians of sexual difference, such as Hélène Cixous and Luce Irigaray. Hélène Cixous's *L'écriture féminine* sexualizes discursive practices and sees the act of writing as subversive, insofar as it allows women to emerge from the phallocratic order that has condemned them to silence. Writing becomes the body, and the body becomes writing, emphasizing difference. Writing becomes the act of giving birth to something that is one with the body, even if not in a biological sense, but in the form of construct and memory, historically determined. The female genderized being becomes, through the mediating maternal relation, a function of writing. Cixous's interpretation, however, does not take into account the different positioning that characterizes actual women who write.

The connection with the mother in association with a creation of a symbolic order from and for women is also part of Luce Irigaray's reflection on the body. Forgetting their origin and detaching themselves from the maternal body has caused men to strive to create worlds for themselves, which compensates them for this loss through the construction of that which is essential to masculinity: language. Everything men produce seems characterized by the repression of the body as the "original dwelling place" that preceded their coming into the world, a repression that influences their mental horizons, their poetry, their way of communicating, and their notion of divine authority. By not seeing themselves as "flesh," originating from the female body, men have submitted this genealogical element to the male one. Thus, in patriarchal society, father-son relationships are favored over mother-daughter relationships. On the contrary, the reconstruction of female genealogies and the sexualized body is related to the formation of a subjectivity and identity based on sexual difference, produced by discursive effects and meaning, which are embodied in the social practices of mediation among women. Western patriarchal culture has always ignored the peculiarity of the female body, capable of giving birth to both sexes.[1]

This is a far cry from a purely biological interpretation of the materiality of the female body that comprises an idea of tolerance in the physical sense, but is also able to express and represent sexual difference as a constitutive element of the female being, starting from oneself.

> Sexual difference, writes Irigaray, cannot be reduced to a simple extralinguistic natural fact. It permeates the language and is permeated by it. . . But patriarchal societies have reduced the value of the female body to such a

> point that its reality and its description of the world is imprecise. Thus, instead of being a different gender, the "woman" has become in our languages the "non-man" or an abstract nonexistent reality [. . .] this explains why women have so much difficulty speaking and being listened to per se. Women have been excluded and denied by the patriarchal linguistic order.[2]

Also alien to a naturalistic vision of the body are the theoretical elaborations of Teresa de Lauretis as well as Donna Haraway's provocative cyborgs. These responses, however, are better suited than the "culture of sexual difference" to the need for knowledge to be partial insofar as, by overcoming the old dichotomy nature-culture implicit in the sex-gender dualism, they see gender as the product and process of social and biomedical technologies, which turn the body into a constructible entity. The body is no longer the inaccessible site of "sexual difference," a difference that, by drawing its borders, gives it a fixed and heavy location to the capacities of representing and narrating it. Differences take the place of difference, acquiring an unstable and multiple character, which is independent of universal designs and teleological knowledge. The biological teleology of the sciences is rejected, and one moves in an interconnected and inhomogeneous social space, within which the semiotic and material representation that defines gender constructs a female subject of feminism that is multiple, contradictory in its meanings, and mobile in its positions. This changes the meaning of communication and of social relations: the representation of class, racial, or sexual identities becomes contradictory by definition, as de Lauretis states, or absolutely partial and provisional, as in the case of the cyborg. The latter human-machine metaphor, as suggested by Haraway, expresses an irreversible crisis of the matrix of identity, which moves in the direction of the posthuman and of the hybridization with the machine. The fleshiness of the body is no longer human or animal, i.e., organic, but extends to the mechanical and inorganic. Following Latour's polemic against epistemological reductionism and purity, which he defines as the "poison of the soul," Haraway introduces the notion of the "apparatus of bodily production," according to which the body is no longer a *tabula rasa,* i.e., passive object appropriated and penetrated by patriarchal knowledge, but an *agent* in the production of new knowledge reference points. Haraway takes this definition from Katie King, who speaks of the *apparatus of literary production* as the source of literature. King uses this definition to designate the emergence of what is "embodied" in this discipline at the intersection of art, economy, and technology, and applies it to the relation between women and writing technologies. Haraway, moving to a different field, refers to the "generation, i.e., the actual production and re-production" of bodies in epistemological knowledge. The body and other "objects" studied by biological sciences become—through that which Haraway calls the maneuver of situated knowledges—active elements, "agents/actors" in the scientific field. This allows one to overcome the dualistic forms characteristic of the traditional epistemological model, which relies on binarisms such as nature/culture and body/mind. The body as the "object of biological discourse" changes its ontological presence from being a passive and exploited resource to that of *agent* lacking a specific identity. Its "factual" and "organic" dimension is translated into that of "semiotic-material actor," i.e., an active object of knowledge, whose boundaries materialize in communicative relations and are mapped out in social practices. In this perspective, there are no preexisting objects with fixed borders. Boundaries are situated within the "objects" themselves, according to their location, and what they contain is the capacity to produce meanings and bodies.

Bodies, therefore, are no longer generated through an internal harmony that delimits them once they are formed, nor do they correspond to univocal and monocentric hierarchies of sex, race, or class, as in the conception of the universal Romantic nineteenth-century subject. In the current technological mutation, bodies are seen as "codified texts," placed within a control system of communicative engineering of intelligent and dispersed networks, which, having overcome the view of the body as organic and monolocational, turn biomedical discourses and knowledges into the main tool of their theoretical and practical positioning. Thus, biotechnical bodies are meaning producing semiotic systems of biomedical discourse. Their boundaries must be liberated from organic constrictions that limit their possibilities and must be seen in terms of assembling and disassembling, without being subject to "natural architectures," which would define them once and for all. It is necessary to concentrate on the fluidity of the boundaries of both bodies and knowledges, rather than on the concept of natural integrity. Cyborgs as embodiments of this multidimensionality and of mobile locations, represent the trespassing of the boundaries of the human, whose laws and biological and cultural status, from modernity onward, have been the main focus of the creation and definition of power relations. Writes Haraway:

> Bodies, then, are not born; they are made. Bodies have been as thoroughly denaturalized as sign, context, and time. Late twentieth-century bodies do not

> grow from internal harmonic principles theorized within Romanticism. Neither are they discovered in the domains of realism and modernism. One is not born a woman, Simone de Beauvoir correctly insisted . . . one is not born an organism. Organisms are made; they are constructs of a world-changing kind. The construction of an organism's boundaries, the job of discourses of immunology, are particularly potent mediators of the experiences of sickness and death for industrial and post-industrial people. . . . Bodies as objects of knowledge are material-semiotic generative nodes. . . . [T]he body ceases to be a stable map of normalized functions and instead emerges as a highly mobile field of strategic differences. (211) . . . One should expect control strategies to concentrate on the boundary conditions and interfaces, on rates of flow across boundaries, not on the integrity of natural objects. . . . No objects, spaces, or bodies are sacred in themselves; any component can be interfaced with any other if the proper standard, the proper code can be constructed for processing signals in a common language. . . . The cyborg is text, machine, body and metaphor—all theorized and engaged in practice in terms of communications. (212)[3]

This trespassing of the boundaries of human nature does not entail an unconditional and acritical celebration of progress and scientific instruments, nor the production of hybrid forms for the purpose of creating omnipotent entities of an infinite perfection, bordering on the transhuman. Currents of thought such as these do exist, especially in the United States, for example in the so-called extropic philosophies, which seek, through nanotechnology and biogenetic engineering, to provide an outlet for their creative anxiety for perfection and unlimited growth, achieving an integration of human and mechanical elements that modify genetic codes. But these efforts are nothing other than the reproposition of anxieties of domination and of the fear of losing control, typical of a patriarchal culture obsessed by the fear of losing its identity under the ceaseless bombardment of infospheric communication, which transforms social relations and the interactive codes of man and machine.

Haraway's effort, on the contrary, with the localization of kinds of knowledge and the partiality attributed to them, moves in the opposite direction. She accepts the epochal transformation we are undergoing, though with some reservation, and actively reacts to it, changing the epistemological status within which the body is defined and located. Thus, she accepts the prospect of mutation but not the indiscriminate use of techno-scientific instruments capable of producing, through a mimetic process of superhuman creation, organisms that manifest their desire for immortality through an omnipotent voracity for seeing and knowing. Haraway's goal is not to imitate the creative power of God. On the contrary, her main purpose is to destabilize locations that define these new entities as elements that help to restructure the communicative processes within the genetic and linguistic code. For Haraway language and technology are closely connected; the idea of "construct" belongs both to the theoretical and social practice as well as to writing, reading, and meaning in the communication process. Technology, body, and semiosis are influenced reciprocally and thus influence the sciences as well as the anthropological and social disciplines.[4]

Also Mario Perniola's "thing that feels" implies a nonnaturalistic view of the body. It goes beyond the borders of what is defined and leads us into the experiential field of transition, where there are no fixed and final points, and the limits of physicality are overcome. By merging philosophy and sexuality, Perniola produces a human sensibility liberated from the verticality and instrumentality of male orgasm and makes it an "artifice," which renders horizontal the increase in feeling. All the nuances of such feeling, made up of sensitivities, conjunctions, and seams are concentrated on the surface of the sensorial organs, which are enhanced to their maximum. It is the same notion of "porosity" found in Stoic philosophy, says Perniola, which uses the sense of touch to suggest something going deeper than mere surface contact. In sexualizing philosophy and desexualizing pleasure, Perniola turns the sex appeal of the inorganic into an element going beyond sensory appearances "in an infinite indicating and denying," which is closer to a female sensibility, horizontal, multidimensional, and capable of multiple orgasms. Perniola, however, abolishes orgasm and defines pleasure as the exact opposite of "the thing that feels," thus going beyond the boundaries of the human body and situating his theory in the field of the inorganic. The shift to this new domain is interesting because one must not be within what is considered "normality," i.e., having a physical disadvantage, or, as Perniola states, of practicing philosophy, or both things together. It is the idea of letting oneself be excited by forms of feeling that are considered inadequate, "perverse," created by unusual stimuli such as numbers, spaces, or objects, which turns us into a thing. In a very amusing essay by Kathy Acker, "Against Ordinary Language: The Language of the Body," the author speaks of her daily body building practice in which her visual and linguistic forms of expression are reduced to a limited number of repetitive exercises. The author says that the beauty and attraction of this discipline, serving to model one's body, lies precisely in the limited and "defective" form of communication it requires. This different feeling consists in assuming the dimension of a "thing." According to Perniola, the fluidity of the identity of the "thing that feels" derives precisely from the capacity to deny any gesture or act that would imprison the spirit or the body in a fixed and heavy identity.[5] The body becomes a fabric, inorganic tissue, the site of a sexuality that dominates the abyss of time because it is always available. Perniola's idea reproposes a view of tactile sensibility for which the skin is like a tissue that covers the body. The skin, with its *orifices* and its *pockets,* marks the boundaries of the body, as Didier Anzieu notes, and entirely wraps the body and the senses, reversing the relation between outside and inside, between ourselves and others. The skin also has a memory that allows it to record past shocks and activate its defenses. Having become the container of the body, it seems increasingly exposed today, not simply naked, but a place of inscriptions and signs: tattooed, pierced, painted; in a word, *wired* in order to achieve durability, denying the unavoidable transitory nature of the body.

The same skin on which Eve, the main character in Emily Prager's novel *Eve's Tattoo,* has the number of a Jewish prisoner at Auschwitz tattooed for her fortieth birthday, a token of what happened, a symbol of the desire to remember the Holocaust after the death of the witnesses. Eve wishes to bear forever on her body the proof of Jewishness, which would otherwise become exclusively the expression of a "privileged identity."[6] Throughout the book, the author emphasizes especially the suffering of women who were first courted under that regime, then betrayed and destroyed. Notwithstanding the effort to stay faithful to a story that does not belong to her—Eve is a Christian—every time she is asked the meaning of that tattoo on her wrist, she invents the story of a different woman, a story improvised on the spot and suited to the moment. Finally, Eve discovers that the number belonged to a Nazi woman, who had landed in the concentration camp by accident, and she understands that those horrendous crimes were perpetrated first of all against the self of each individual, especially female, whether "Aryan" or "Jewish." To have her skin tattooed in the effort to continue to bear witness makes her understand that her stories were better than reality and that memory, in order not to be destroyed, must especially be the signifier of a lack, a communicative mutilation, going beyond belonging, rather than the constantly present memory of a model identity. The skin then becomes the object of transitory communicative signals that do not aspire to the corruptible eternity of the body. For example, in the case of the cyborg artist Stelarc, those signals take the form of electrical shocks and sensors that, through their communicative position on the skin, reveal the extreme precariousness and at the same time the constructability of the body.

The virtual sexuality of Perniola's philosophical, sexual cyborg, therefore, through the sensorial and inactive intensification of tactility, manifests a willingness to be permanently aroused. Writes Perniola: "The body which has neutral sexuality is not a machine but a *fabric.* It is made up of numerous types of material overlapping and interwoven. Giving oneself as a *thing that feels* means asking that our partners' fabrics mix with ours creating a single extension in which we travel for hours, for days. Thus, the difference between giving and taking disappears: a foreign body, or better a fabric appears. It belongs to no one."[7]

The encounter of two "sentient things" is not destined, therefore, to create a stable, well-defined form. For Perniola, as for Haraway, it is necessary to abandon the fullness and harmony of self-reflection and self-sufficiency in idealist and romantic thought. This philosophy viewed individuals as fixed entities, satisfied and content with their belonging and limitations, self-oriented and self-contained, hostile to any transformation. To these, Perniola opposes the emptiness that underlies the neutral sexuality of the "thing that feels." The sex-appeal of the inorganic, from this perspective, is the product of a "porous thought," which does not stay within safe methodological limits and is always becoming something other than itself; it is also literature, no less than a theory of society, no less than the history of ideas, or also sexology and philosophy.[8]

This experience leads to transition, the transformation from one thing into another, from one knowledge into another, without ever having to define the boundary between inside and outside. It is precisely philosophy that has the role of propagating this experience, the experience of bodies without difference, where the outside is "surface, skin, fabric."

If, on the one hand, I understand Perniola's critique of Haraway's cyborg, whom he sees as too dependent on "human normality," modified through mechanical devices, too close to what he defines as a "simulated sensorial deprivation," on the other hand, I fear this effort to desexualize pleasure, totally eliminating the moment of orgasm. The beauty of turning the experience of performance into a tool for manipulating the reality we have inherited must be weighed against the fact that when one enters the domain of the inorganic, this happens at the expense of the body, which becomes a sort of empty container capable of infinitely expanding its sensitive performance by totally overcoming the limitations of the physical world and abolishing all differences between reality and its imitation. For Perniola the question is not one of lightening or evading reality, but of entering a different dimension, where the ontological boundaries between reality and its representation become blurred and performance is not competitive, insofar as it is not directed towards the oppression of someone else but towards entrance into the inorganic world we have become. But I fear the idea of going beyond the body, implicit in the above position, that is supported by the sexualization of philosophy as a "perverse" manifestation of a handicap due to the inability of providing instruments of social representation. If, on the one hand, the idea of "porosity" is intriguing, harking us back to the transition from one "thing" to another, to the experiment of trespassing the boundaries of knowledges, the materiality of the body and feelings, then, on the other hand, I am perplexed about the sexualization of philosophy. In desexualizing pleasure and the body, philosophy would end up expressing the age old desire for immortality, albeit inverted. The body is removed from the assaults of time and is situated in the domain of the inorganic where its capacity "to feel" is a source of "endless wonder." What raises my doubts about the *cold* provocations of Donna Haraway's cyborg and Perniola's "thing that feels" is not the fact that they both seek, even if in very different ways, to go beyond the boundaries of the preestablished and the organic, recreating the idea of nature or modifying the role of feeling. On the contrary, I find this effort stimulating and original. Rather, I find disturbing the sensation that these entities lack the warm flow that should be created by the transformations they must undergo in order to become what they are.

Instead, it seems important to me to focus attention on the process of passing, which, if it is to let us into the artificial and mechanical world, must take us beyond the borders of the known, into warm phases of fluidity that would serve to increase its transitory condition rather than allow us to reach a final destination. The blurring and trespassing of the boundaries between languages, knowledges, and communication, cause mutations that undermine stable structures and require desiring energies suffused with heat. Therefore, rather than discussing "objects" or "things" capable of transforming "knowledges" and "sensibilities," I wish to emphasize, as a sign of change, the process of dissolution of identity boundaries that these designate and cross.

Incidentally, I wonder whether the fear of the warm flow and of the conjunction of corporeal fluids generated by AIDS, does not influence our collective imagination, unconsciously determining the repression of all elements of fluidity. It seems to me that there is a tendency, even in intellectuals who elaborate original and stimulating analyses, to bring attention to bear on a condition of asepticness, coldness, and the neutrality of the body that serves to immunize sexuality from the terror of viral infection. Certainly, the immunological research that has developed in consequence of the spread of AIDS continuously expands the boundaries of what is known and, at the same time, the biological limits of our genetic inheritance. The danger and fear of contagion have become constant companions, influencing social and sexual behaviors. The values of chastity and purity along with a growing fear of heterogeneity and diversity are commonly found among the young.

Scientific discoveries also influence common language and social behavior. Thus, while twenty-years ago Italian dictionaries did not mention "ecological" as a synonym of "clean," nowadays the antonyms of this word are often associated with the notion of contamination, corruption, guilt, obscenity, and illegality, which previously had a secondary role or were completely absent. Likewise, the idea of decay and physical contagion is linked to terms with a moral, normative meaning. A disease caused by sexual contact, such as AIDS, becomes an element that breaks the original contract on which the stability and normality of sexual and social behaviors are based. It is a taboo that breaks ethical codes of behavior and the inflexibility of the law. At the start, at least in Western countries, AIDS affected only the homosexual community and heroine addicts, two minority groups that could be easily isolated even more than previously. But when the contagion spread to the world of heterosexuals and nonaddicts, then the disease became a common threat, not only because it affected all social groups, but because it gave visibility to previously marginalized subjects and to their relation with the "normal" world, thus opening a fissure in the rigidity of the binary sexual system and in petite-bourgeois moralism. Though a proper linguistic study of this topic would require a much more detailed semiological investigation, it is evident that dictionaries record changes that are the product of the alteration of the boundaries of words and social behaviors as signifiers. For this reason, it is necessary, more than ever, that the concepts of fluid transition, vulnerability (as opposed to power or infinity), ironical evasion, and impure hybridity (as opposed to aggressiveness or sterilized neutrality) become the main characteristics of the new entities being constructed, whether *cyborgs* or *things that feel.* Passing is the tool we need to avoid the risk of a new law that would ensnare us again in the oppressive and solid confines of normative rigidity. Passing is animated by the same need for irony and provocation that we find in the *outlaw bodies* mentioned by Arthur and Marilouise Kroker.[9] In the effort to escape the heaviness and the unbreakability of the norms of sexual binarism, these bodies have changed sex, or have experienced a transgenderism that turns mutation into an element of subversion of norm and normality. This is the last sex for whom the fluidity of identity boundaries is a daily project. Women belong to it by definition because, within the normative structure of patriarchal sexual dualism, they pass from the centrality of the age of sexual harassment to the margins of the age of invisibility that appears with the first wrinkle. The temporal framework we are caught in produces a process of gradual disappearance into a representation of male imagination that has been imposed on us. Moving contradictorily, as suggested by Teresa de Lauretis, between the space of that representation and that which it leaves out, i.e., in the *space off,* we see how that process belongs to all the subjects that rebel against a law that seeks to mummify identity codes and limit their subversive impact on the heterosexual contract. The last sex includes all those who have no fear of going beyond the boundaries of the closed world of binary sexuality and who wish to avoid any drive for purity and for the preservation of sexual, ethnic, racial, or corporeal belonging. That form of preservation, as the Krokers suggest, is nothing but "a new form of cultural fascism, with its nostalgic defense of pure referents that never existed and its panic-fear about a dirty world."[10]

And, of course, it is this "dirty world" that *The Last Sex* is interested in. Besides Elisabeth Rodger's beautiful photos of female bodies placed within a frame that emphasizes their vulnerability and the image of their erased identities, the book contains stories of women tormented by the heaviness of their bodies. Violence, sadomasochistic pleasures, gender changes, and technological hybridization, are the themes of the stories in this book, which turns irony into the main narrative tool. Already on the cover we find the photo of a very sexy woman dressed as a bride, bearing the caption "Men are dumb. I know I've been one." What those who belong to the last sex have in common, the authors state, are thus three things: the rejection of predetermined categories, a provocative insistence on political commitment (only the sort that privileges the categories of ambivalence, irony, and paradox), and refusal of any single position or reference taken as a limit or arrival point. The last sex knows no barriers, it attacks all types of purity and stable origins. There is a constant fluctuation that never reaches a normative conclusion. It is the centrality of the transition that Heléna Velena, in her *Dal cybersex al transgender* sees as the fundamental element of a new way of experiencing sexuality that never accepts the idea of a starting point or a final destination, questioning all binary structures. Velena writes: "[I]f the transition exists two precise moments could be missing: the place from and the place to. The problem is that it is exactly this transition which should be the practice. Transition as movement, as transformation not transformism; as mutation not as recycling."[11]

The transgenderism mentioned by the author, therefore, goes beyond binary sexuality and leads to various different possible identities, toward the modification of one's body through technology, as an essential moment of experimentation and exploration, capable of liberating desiring and subversive energies, forever moving without ever fixing a final destination.

Passing

"MONKEY SEE, MONKEY DO" IS THE ENGLISH EXPRESSION USED TO describe the behavior of a person, a child usually, who mimics the behavior of someone else. "To ape" indicates something similar, the mimetic attitude that is ascribed to simians: a mechanical conditioned reflex, independent of rational volition and incapable of an articulated, autonomous elaboration of memories, the mere repetition of actions performed or imposed by others.

"See no evil, hear no evil, speak no evil" is another expression used to indicate the behavior of the three monkeys, symbolizing the impossibility to communicate and the intention to perpetuate dominant social narratives and behaviors through a conniving silence. It is the principle of the "omertà" of the Mafia that demands absolute subservience to a system of power and domination, whose rigidly hierarchical structure lives and is transmitted thanks to a blind faith in the organization and a renunciation of any personal initiative. Its members, like so many monkeys, follow their leaders and execute orders, without ever interfering or questioning them, never committing a betrayal. Silence becomes connivance, the protection and reproduction of the system and its methods. Such was the case in the system of power and complicity that made corruption and cronyism a daily operating method, in the recruitment of new adepts in Italian political life for more than forty years.

"Monkeying around," on the other hand, is a slang expression used to indicate an attitude of excessive playfulness, an irresponsible attitude, lacking due seriousness.

This animal species (monkeys), so disturbingly similar to our own species, stimulates all sorts of unconscious fears. It has been used and abused to indicate the condemnation of automatic mimicry as well as of irresponsibility and, at the same time, the danger that these attitudes represent for the human race: the danger of repeating past mistakes. Thus, monkeys represent the slumber of reason, animality *versus* humanity, the opposite of historical memory, blind response that does not learn from past events and is condemned to mechanically commit the same errors over and over again. In a sense, the monkey is the opposite of the Hegelian mole, which, as a symbol of historical awareness, represents the social forces that work beneath the surface of society to emerge when the time is ripe. The mole cannot see because it is blind but cannot be seen because it lives and works *underground.* It is for this reason that when it emerges, it has the advantage of surprise. But today in our visual culture, where nothing can surprise us, what use can such an animal have, if not that of tying us to the past and turning the underground world into one of rage and resentment?

It is also interesting to retrace the association between the term *monkey* and the use of alcohol or heroin, as in "a monkey on one's back," to signify the loss of control over reason and memory that some see as a transition to a state of vegetation, characterized by the absence of communication, while others take it for an expansion of visionary and psychedelic powers. Yet the *monkey* bears no relation, at least no linguistic one, with the psychochemical world of *smart drugs* that serve to increase the memory and acumen of individuals and are the deliberate expression of a desire for omnipotence.

The monkey is also used for immunobiological experiments because of its being the bearer of viral and bacteriological diseases that are sometimes lethal for humankind. Reduced to a dangerous subspecies, like the androids in *Blade Runner* who say, "We're stupid, we're destined to die," these ancestors of humankind would seem destined to play a secondary role in the collective *image repertoire* or to remain confined within the banality of negative stereotypes. On the contrary, in the most recent productions of artists, but also of philosophers and scientists, monkeys have become the object of a new curiosity as signifiers of an interfacing with technology that raises disturbing questions about the future of the human race and its parallel relation to the machine. For example, the word *monkey* is sometimes used, as in "monkey's virus," to indicate a pathological agent that alters the normal and "healthy" functioning of the computer and erases its memory, destroying or damaging stored information.

The monkey is a disturbing symbol of our relationship with progress and history, exposing all that is inescapably fragile, mortal, and enigmatic in the human condition.

Reversing the evolutionary principle that causes us to retrace our ancestry backwards to them in order to ascertain our origin, these animals, who represent our genetic and historical background, have a disquieting and ambiguous role that escapes the dominant models of narration and social experience, and can be taken as a symbol of our future. Donna

Haraway has long studied the habits of apes as the basis for a redefinition of our ideas of nature and social ties and, in general, has focused on figures that question the traditional structure of technological, biological, and historical Western knowledge, such as monkeys, women, and cyborgs. And what about the paradoxical and amusing contest between Frank Curzio, one of the most successful Wall Street brokers, and a monkey, named Casey, which started in 1994, and up to now has the monkey leading by far with profits that sometimes amount to ten times those of one of the most famous and extravagant New York executives? In movies such as Kubrick's *2001: A Space Odyssey,* Kusturica's *Underground,* and Gilliam's *12 Monkeys,* among others, these mammals symbolize in different forms the evolution of *téchne,* the abandonment of a past of hatreds, and the development of biological sciences, respectively.

In the lyrics of Roger Waters, former member of Pink Floyd, monkeys are the protagonists of a Big Brother scenario where, thanks to television, the human species becomes extinct. *Amused to Death,* the 1992 CD, is very close in title and content to Neil Postman's *Amusing Ourselves to Death.* Both authors, in the wake of Aldous Huxley's *Brave New World,* are alarmed by the possibility that, through a complete surrender to entertainment, people may sink into apathy, losing their ability to think and feel. The technological medium, television in this case, represents a diabolical form of addiction that anesthetizes feelings and desire, without forcing the individual's will. The figure of the monkey, as used by Waters, is a complex symbol both of the absence of memory and the lack of interest caused by familiarity with technology and of the people's need to legitimate the inevitable progress of history. In his beautiful piece, *Watching TV,* which recounts the events of Tiananmen Square in China, Waters presents the death of a young student in terms of the universality of a brotherhood, which, through the images of the woman's sacrifice, broadcasted all over the world, tragically warns us against our disinterest for our lost liberty and at the same time symbolically evokes our failure in preserving it. In this context, the monkey symbolizes the justification that, through the written preservation of memory and history, humanity has invented the inevitability of historical events and the consequences of progress:

> The monkey looked at the stars
> and thought of himself
> Memory it's a stranger
> History is for fools

He cleaned his hands
in a pool of sacred writing
he turned his back on the garden
and left for the nearest town . . .
time is linear.

In the lyric, written language becomes the instrument for liberating the guilty feelings that a particular direction and conception of progress and scientific development have produced, as well as serving to replicate an omnivorous and linear time. In this sense, the monkey is the devastating symbol of a catastrophe that is already underway. By writing history the monkey unifies the parallel stories of different communities and subjects within an empty time and universal space, destroying all impediments to the unrestrained march of the idea of progress, which leads to the final disaster and the erasure of diverse forms of alterity. In the title song, Waters imagines a future where our lifeless planet will be visited by alien anthropologists who will investigate the reason for our extinction. The only possible explanation they can find is the fact that our species proved incapable of detaching its entertained shadow from TV. People developed a universal indifference that furthered the process of extinction. Having lost the ability to communicate, human beings laughed themselves into oblivion, without even knowing why they were laughing.

Two psychoanalysts, Michael White and David Epston, have also insisted on the importance of the combination of written and oral languages as alternative tools of expression, allowing us to renarrate ourselves in different stories, which disappeared into the dominant and repetitive narration that we carry inside. White and Epston insist on the need for a psychological shift, both social and individual, in our way of communicating. While working in two different countries, Australia and New Zealand respectively, they have concentrated on a common goal, that of opening new horizons in the perception of the self through their professional experience in family therapy. Two discoveries are fundamental to their work. First of all there is the "externalization of the problem" as an entity separate and distinct from the individual who is the bearer of the problem, in contrast with the great majority of psychoanalytic practices that tend to merge the two. This means that the focus is on the interaction between people and the problems that arise within this interaction. This goes to the heart of individual identity, which is constituted by what we know of ourselves and how we describe ourselves as individuals. In most cases this is defined, at least in psychoanalysis, by cultural practices (describing, naming, classifying, evaluating, isolating, excluding, etc.) in which we are imprisoned. As human beings, our linguistic expressions are dominated by invisible forms of control that these practices activate and by implicit sociocultural models of coordination. If those around us, for example, believe that we have certain given characteristics or problems, they exert power over us through the representation of this knowledge. Thus, methods that in the social sphere, according to the Foucaltian notion of knowledge-power used by the two psychoanalysts, were techniques that disempowered individuals and empowered problems, in the therapy sessions are used to "externalize the problem." The second important discovery is the use of written language in therapeutic practice, i.e., letters, certificates, invitations, references, that are never used, however, as objective descriptions of fact. They serve instead to bring to light distinctions having heuristic value, since they are connected to specific experiences and significant events, from which stories can be produced, having the power to highlight the problem and further its solution. Common words are used in unusual ways to charter on paper the evolution of the problem and its outcomes. While the preference of the two scientists goes to oral language, in line with the psychoanalytic tradition, there is an emphasis on the written medium because "it facilitates the mapping of experience onto the temporal dimension [and] has much to offer to those activities defined as therapy [. . .] and provides one with a mechanism through which persons can be more active in determining the arrangement of information and experience and in producing different accounts of events and experience."[1] This generates a new form of experience that stimulates the imagination and the reader's participation in the text. Through the analogy between therapy and narrative text, the two psychoanalysts turn therapy into a process of *historicization* or rather *rehistoricization* of the lives and experiences of patients. The narratives through which people describe their lives determine their social interactions and their experiences. The evolution of their existence and of their relationships is expressed through their stories and the way they tell them. Thus the analogy between text and therapy is different from other analogical *topoi,* which are usually limited to the identification of the structure and pathology of such narratives. However, the evolution of the lives and relationships of the patients, as expressed through the *performance* of the stories, refers instead to the relative indeterminacy present in all texts. The existence of an implicit meaning in the perspective of each different reading of given events and the existence of different types of metaphors for the description of those events impart a degree of ambiguity to every story.

With each *performance* the patients re-authorize their lives. Thus, the analogy with the text inserts us into an intertextual world in two ways: first the lives of people are situated in texts that are in turn part of other texts and second, through its *performance,* each narration or renarration of a story becomes a new story that incorporates and develops the former one. When power techniques have been identified through an investigation of the episodes in which people subjugated themselves or others through the repetition of a given story, it becomes possible to identify what White and Epston call "unique outcomes."

These allow patients to externalize the problem, to identify alternative solutions, and to represent new meanings through the medium of performance. In this way, patients are liberated from those forms of power-knowledge that constrained them and that tended to reproduce themselves without leaving room for alternative stories, for vital aspects of their past experience that had been neglected.

Through the documentation of events and ideas "in black and white," the letters and therapeutic certificates that are produced contribute in a very material sense to the cocreation of new liberating narratives. This analogy has a great intuitive appeal and serves to infuse liveliness and significance into the narratives people produce. The analogy with the written text also serves to bridge the distance between the area of narrative media and that of knowledge as power. Not only do we attribute significance to the experience of historicizing our lives, we *authorize* ourselves, i.e., we give ourselves the authority to become again authors and to represent our stories through our direct knowledge of them.

The stories thus produced are the product of different sources. People have various stories about themselves, others and their relations with them. Furthermore, other stories can be reassuring, liberating, and therapeutic. The particular story that prevails over others in giving meaning to the events of our lives determines the main characteristics of our experience and becomes the model for our future behavior. When a story "saturates" a problem, its dominion becomes oppressive and we fall into depression. Given the conservative tendency that characterizes us, it becomes increasingly difficult to liberate ourselves from the constant, obsessive repetition of the old problematic story. It is the presence of problematic knowledge and the prevalence of pathological stories that make the investigation of knowledge as power relevant. White and Epston's formulation, through its externalization, makes the problem into an individual entity with a life of its own. By using the written medium to record the moment when the dominant pattern is broken, they suggest the possibility of rearranging and renarrating the elements of the narration of the self into new stories that would emphasize previously neglected elements, offering alternative "outcomes" to the old pattern and possible solutions to the problem.

The rediscovery of the importance of linear time through written language provides the basis for the performance of new stories outside the repetitive pattern of the dominant one. Yet, from my perspective, there is still too much emphasis on the formation of stable stories and entities. Obviously, we are in the field of analytic therapy, where the "solution to the problem" lies in the ability to free the patient from a dominant pathological behavior and secure a final result with a degree of stability, as a defense against the reemergence of the problem. On the one hand, this technique facilitates the dynamics of identity, insofar as it moves toward the acknowledgment of the stratification of different levels in the individual and social identity within which tyrannical impositions force us to repeat the same story and the same representation of the self, at the expense of other stories. On the other, there is an emphasis on the final result, the return to the safe haven of a "sight-centered" tradition, where sight, through the medium of written language, allows us to achieve a stable knowledge and stable interpersonal relations.

On the contrary, it is my belief that other senses must be taken into account in the analysis of practices where dominant narratives and dominant views of social relations are evaded. The testimonial authority attributed to written language over oral language, the prevalence of sight over hearing, must be challenged in the interest of alternative forms of knowledge, and therefore of power, where the fundamental characteristics are no longer formalization, legitimization, continuity, or the ability to *perform.* It is necessary, as in the case of passing to which Nella Larsen refers, to move into a terrain that "is not entirely strange, not entirely friendly," one that is not completely under control and that does not have us under its complete control: the domain of what is not permanent. White and Epson's use of certificates and letters is in line with the absolute domination that written communication is gaining in the digital era (e-mail, newsgroups, and so on) as the privileged mode of deconstructing and restructuring models of knowledge and interpersonal relations, at the expense of other forms of communication. Behind this trend I see a desire for visual reassurance that is too close for comfort to an excessively normative, regulatory, and fixed notion of social relations and communication.

From a theoretical perspective, it is interesting to note how the music field, where technological experimentation has been at the forefront in the last few decades, is the one that has produced the most acute, original, and ironic, though often disturbing, considerations on our present and our future. Music uses electromagnetic waves and sophisticated technology to produce, amplify, and distribute sounds, a hot flow of heterogeneous communicative sources and forms that closely intermingle, combining the human element with the mechanical one to the point that the two become often indistinguishable. It is therefore the medium of communication most suited to the period of technological transition that we are currently experiencing. From this point of view, it is essential to the understanding and practice of passing.

Hakim Bey has argued that the concept of music is a symbol of revolutionary change and becomes the new organizational principle precisely on account of its instability and of its hybridization with technological media.[2] There are musical experiments—especially those focusing on the fusion of technical and the human elements as a strategy for overcoming the man-machine dualism—that, through the use of sophisticated devices, often directly applied to the body, bring out the possibility of constructing the body, questioning its relation to language and turning it into the object of creative and original experiments. David Bowie's CD *Outside,* with the story of a serial killer as its leading motif, is a mixture of bodily and technological interiors; human organs become part of the code that is disassembled and reassembled in a mysterious, disquieting musical language bearing witness to a contemporaneity that locates it outside the narrow boundaries of linear time.

Body, language, and their relation to technology are the subject of the lyrics of another musician, less angst-ridden than Bowie and less apocalyptic than Waters, though wary of uncontrolled scientific developments: Laurie Anderson. For Anderson, too, the monkey is an important and ambivalent symbol. *The American multimediatrix,* as one critic has defined her, has proven her ability to use various sophisticated technological media ironically, without turning them into signifiers of the death of the body or of its omnipotence. In fact, her amused and irreverent approach allows her to produce very sensuous music. From this perspective, the lightness that characterizes women is used by Anderson to escape from stereotypes of gender identity. Anderson is capable of overcoming gender dualisms without turning the body into a neutral element, to elude sexual cliches through a playful variation of roles and functions. For example, the use of the "Vocoder" allows her to alter her voice, and simulate male and female voices, different ages and accents, animal calls, voices, or the sound of objects. In openly placing in the foreground the technological means through which sounds and voices are altered, Anderson highlights the importance of the machine in the production of new sounds, new identities, and, more in general, in the redefinition of linguistic and social relations. Yet there are also dangers at hand. Technology can be a campfire around which we gather to socialize and exchange stories, but one should be wary of being burned. Thus, in the song *Monkey's Paw,* on the CD *Strange Angels* produced in 1989, scientific experimentation does not automatically guarantee us a better future because:

> The Gift of Life It's a Twist of Faith
> It's a Roll of The Dice
> It's a Free Lunch, a Free Ride
> The Gift of Life is a Shot in the Dark
> It's a Call of the Wild
> It's the Big Wheel, the Great Race
> But Nature's Got Rules, Nature's Got Laws
> and if You Enter It Be Careful
> It's a Monkey's Paw
> You Better Stop!
> Look Around!
> Listen!

Words play a major role in Laurie Anderson's music and her sophisticated experimental style also extends to her verses, which are characterized by great poetical intensity. The power of the written word, the traditional hallmark of the more "advanced" Western tradition, is questioned. Notwithstanding the frequent, massive use of complex mediatic tools, in 1995 Anderson produced a CD with a very low technological content—the lowest ever for her—based almost entirely on the spoken word and taken from her book *Stories from the Nerve Bible,* published in 1994. Only a few musical sounds and noises are used, as a background to the public reading of extracts from her book. In the small leaflet enclosed with the CD, Anderson explains that what prompted her to turn her book into a CD was that the written material, the result of twenty years of experimental work, was really meant to be orally narrated. "I believe that language is a living thing," writes Anderson, "and when we listen to something the meaning is completely different from when we see it on the written page. [. . .] Without the special effects of a multimedia show this CD became a sort of mental movie. I felt as if I were in the places I was describing. And I was free to jump and cut—a story of twenty years ago is suddenly side by side with one that happened last week."[3] Time and space, when translated into narrated movie images, lose their diachronic sequential character and give stories back their evocative power based more on desire than on the need for objective truth and linear narration. The last song, *Same Time Tomorrow,* calls the linearity of time into question; it speaks of the West and the East as mental locations rather than points of departure or origin, and of the fact that the spoken language is never an exact rendition of our memories. According to Anderson, many significant stories of our lives of which memory records only partial fragments will never be written, but will exist only in our own personal narration, tied to the image of a lover, a place, or an event. These fragments are powerful mnemonic images, which spring to life once they are narrated. Like Walter Benjamin's *flaneur,* wandering at random through the city and catching glimpses of the past, memory engages everyday in this rediscovery of long-lost fragments, a process that is never fixed in a "dialectic," and diachronic construction of history and is only occasionally translated into writing. This theme is found throughout the CD, *Strange Angels.* In the song entitled *The Dream Before,* dedicated to Walter Benjamin, the artist sees Hansel and Gretel as two characters whom an omnivorous historical memory has constrained within stereotypes that are foreign and stifling to them, and who constantly dream of becoming something different from what they are. The lyric, which echoes the figure of Benjamin's angel of history with its face turned toward the past, warns against history's consuming fury. The same theme pervades the CD taken from the book *Stories from the Nerve Bible,* which Anderson composed with only the use of the violin, Brian Eno, on keyboards, with a few other digital instruments, and personally mixed. The central themes of the CD are narratives that reveal a connection to the spoken word. These compositions have a high sense of spirituality and irony. As Anderson states in one of the first lyrics, the title refers to the Bible because the first stories she heard when she was little were taken from this "strange" text, which spoke about seas opening, animals talking, and in which adults, the one and only source of her sense of reality, had an unshakeable faith. Through these stories, Anderson was introduced to a form of surrealism that later on made it hard for her to distinguish between reality and artistic forms. For this reason, the truth of these stories, which is often the subject of the questions she is asked off stage, is a secondary issue. What is important is to communicate through stories, rather than ascertaining the original truth or the objectivity of the narrative. The common theme in these stories, as Anderson states, is the body, whose parts appear and disappear throughout the book, providing various portraits of people, not particularly realistic, by means of voices and sounds. For example, the title of the CD, *The Ugly One with the Jewels,* composed after a trip to Mexico where Anderson's brother worked as an anthropologist, specifically takes its denomination from the name given to her by the Indios with whom they were staying. She was "ugly" because she diverged from local standards in regards to head-dress and clothing, and the "jewels" were her transparent contact lenses, which every night before going to bed Anderson stored on the shelf while carefully "hiding" them in her eyes during the day. The metaphor of hiding a precious object on the body turns the object into a protective, pulsating entity, both fragile and strong, highlighting its constructability in poetic or rather prosaic, i.e., biological or technological, terms. It is interesting that Anderson chose the metaphor of the eyes as the title for her CD, where the organs of sight are a container of jewels rather than an active instrument of knowledge. In Western society, sight has been the privileged instrument of learning and language the main vehicle of communication and reproduction of a culture and power structure that was the exclusive domain of men, from which women were excluded for a long time. The fact that these organs are given a dimension that highlights the constructability of the body, i.e., its capacity to hide objects that serve to improve sight, serves to bring to the forefront—through the symbolic image repertoire of populations foreign to Western ideas of knowledge and power—their poetic and technological function of protecting a precious good.

Irony and lyrical intensity make Anderson's artistic creations an instrument that goes beyond the stereotypes, actually caricatures, of identities that are a hindrance to individual creativity and expression. It is a passing music, emotional, intense, and alien from any predetermined end, if not that of eliminating barriers to communication between human beings who, through bodies mediated by technology, turn social relations into precarious modes of survival and of profound spiritual meditation. It is the perilous path of experimentation and of the fluctuating and uncertain expression of desire, chosen rather than the safe route of stable identities and affiliations, which we have inherited and, like "monkeys," seek to reproduce. It is the unsafe territory of the encounter with the unknown that forces us to face the fact that vulnerability, precariousness, and a sense of displacement are a necessary part of the contemporary condition. The desperation and resistance that we meet every time we move away from our certainties is perhaps the measure of the failure of our imagination, the limitations from which all racial, religious, class, and sexual prejudices are born.

Passing, which cannot be subject to definitions that seek to turn it into an all-purpose slogan, becomes a synonym of a form of social communication centered on the ironic alteration of the sacredness of the myths of origin and of history, in favor of a subversive game that undermines the centrality of any dominant culture basing its representation and supposed objectivity on such myths. Passing is neither what one does when one performs nor what one is as a subject, but a way of representing and experiencing the fluidity of interpersonal and psycho-political dynamics. It is not a new theory of identity, but an answer to it in terms of *situated* politics. As in Nella Larsen's *Passing,* passing is the theoretical, political linguistic place in which racial, sexual, and class objectives meet. Not having a "safe haven" to return to means—as in the case of women and all those who have been colonized by dominant cultures, economies, or sexual contracts—that passing is something different from passing *from* or passing *for.* It is the precariousness of individual identity, which is not what marks the *other,* but the *self* that each one of us considers as his or her own. Therefore, passing does not aspire to be a universal value, but is determined through a communicative and social positioning of the knowledges and cultures to which, as individuals, we refer. The superseding of linguistic, ethnic, religious, racial, and gender barriers must be removed from the models of rationality or acquired knowledge by giving in to the fascination of travelling, of "navigating" without a fixed destination, which from the distant Homeric hero has been transmitted, through countless alterations, all the way down to the age of computers. By interacting—albeit in a wary fashion, refusing to take all change for granted—with the technology that universalizes and actualizes infospheric communication, we help further this process. It is not possible to perform passing by claiming a subjectivity, a body, or a real and authentic dimension. As members of a network of virtual communities, for example, where we can temporarily and with a degree of anonymity simulate a variety of identities through which we can contact other individuals, we need to articulate fluid cultural and mediatic attitudes. In other words, the attitudes of passing, which—like the Indian chief Hiawatha in Laurie Anderson's song, who taught the Iroquois the arts of magic and navigation—can move at ease both on the route of the stars and along fiber optic cables. "The wild, sky blue waters of the shining Big Sea," the ones where the encounter with the uncertainty of the unknown and of that which we seek to become, takes place is where passing finds its preferred location.

Notes

Preface

1. See Samira Kawash, "*The Autobiography of an Ex-Colured Man:* (Passing for) Black Passing for White," *in Passing and Fictions of Identity,* edited by Elaine Ginsberg (Durham: Duke University Press, 1996).

2. Juda Bennett, "Toni Morrison and the Burden of Passing Narrative," *African American Review,* vol. 35, no. 2 (Summer, 2001): 206.

3. Edmund Morgan, *American Slavery, American Freedom: The Ordeal of Colonial Virginia* (New York, 1975).

4. Maria Giulia Fabi, *Passing and the Rise of the African American Novel* (Chicago: University of Illinois Press, 2001), 4.

5. Gunnar Myrdal, *An American Dilemma: The Negro Problem and modern Democracy* (New York: Harper and Row, 1962), 683.

6. Samira Kawash, *Dislocating the Color Line: Identity, Hybridity, and Singularity in African-American Literature* (Stanford: Stanford University Press, 1997), 126–27.

7. James Ernest Conyers, "Selected Aspect of the Phenomenon of Negro Passing." Ph. D. dissertation, Washington, 1962: 317. Quoted in Samira Kawash, *Dislocating the Color Line: Identity, Hybridity, and Singularity in African-American Literatur*e (Stanford: Stanford University Press, 1997), 127.

8. Conyers, "Selected Aspect of the Phenomenon of Negro Passing," 37. Quoted in Samira Kawash, *Dislocating the Color Line: Identity, Hybridity, and Singularity in African-American Literature,* 127.

9. For more on this issue, see Daryl Michael Scott, *Contempt & Pity: Social Policy and the Image of the Damaged Black Psyche 1880–1996* (Chapel Hill: The University of North Carolina Press, 1997).

10. Phillip Brian Harper, "Passing for What? Racial Masquerade and the Demands of Upward Mobility," *Callaloo,* vol. 21, no. 2 (Spring 1989): 381.

11. Samira Kawash, *Dislocating the Color Line: Identity, Hybridity, and Singularity in African-American Literature,* 124–25.

12. Ibid., 134.

13. Linda Schlossberg, "Introduction: Rites of Passing," in *Passing: Identity and Interpretation in Sexuality, Race and Religion,* edited by Maria Carla Sanchez and Linda Schlossberg, (New York: New York University Press, 2001), 1.

14. Ibid., 128.

15. Kathleen Pfeiffer, *Race passing and American Individualism* (Boston: University of Massachusetts Press, 2003), 3.

16. Ibid., 2.

17. Werner Sollors, *Neither Black nor White yet Both* (New York: Oxford University Press, 1997), 250.

18. Gayle Wald, *Crossing the Line* (Durham: Duke University Press, 2000), 7.

19. Ibid., 9.

20. Cheryl Wall, "Passing for What? Aspects of Identity in Nella Larsen's Novels," *Black American Literature Forum,* vol. 20, no. 1 and 2 (Spring–Summer 1986):105.

21. Ibid., 105.

22. Elaine Ginsberg, "Introduction: The Politics of Passing," in *Passing and Fictions of Identity,* edited by Elaine Ginsberg (Durham, NC: Duke University Press, 1996), 4.

23. Charles Scruggs's review of *Passing and Fictions of Identity* in *American Literature,* vol. 69, no. 3, (September 1997): 639–40.

24. Carol Wilson's review of *Passing and Fictions of Identity, The Journal of Southern History,* vol. 64, no. 1 (February 1989): 160.

25. Pamela Caughie, *Passing and Pedagogy: The Dynamics of Responsibility* (Urbana: University of Illinois, 1999), 2.

26. Samira Kawash, *Dislocating the Color Line: Identity, Hybridity, and Singularity in African-American Literature,* 147.

Introduction

1. Aldo Gargani, editor, *Crisi della ragione* (Turin: Einaudi, 1979), 8.

2. Carla Lonzi, *Sputiamo su Hegel* Milan, *Scritti di rivolta feminile,* 1974, 34.

3. Ibid., 43.

4. Franco Berardi (Bifo), *Neuormagma. Lavoro cognitivo e infoproduzione* (Rome: Castelvecchi, 1995), 10.

My Point of View

1. Original text.

2. Dick Hebdige, *Subculture: The Meaning of Style* (London and New York, 1988), 148.

3. Ibid., 16–17.

4. Ibid., 17.

The Feminist Trail

1. Original text.

2. Carla Lonzi, *Sputiamo su* Hegel, 17–18.

3. Diotma, *Il pensiero della differenza sessuale* (Milan: La Tartaruga, 31).

4. Rosi Braidotti, *Nomadic Subjects, Embodiment and Sexual difference in Contemporary Feminist Theory* (Columbia University Press, New York, 1994), p. 169.

5. Braidotti, *Soggetto nomade,* 158.

6. Braidotti, *Soggetto nomade,* 165.

7. Ibid., 170.
8. Ibid., 171.
9. Ibid., 133.
10. Ibid., 131.
11. Ibid., 40.
12. Ibid.
13. Ibid., 94.
14. Teresa De Lauretis, *Technologies of Gender* (Bloomington and Indianapolis: Indiana University Press, 1987), 3.
15. Ibid., 25.
16. Ibid., 26.
17. Donna Haraway, *Simians, Cyborgs, and Women: The reinvention of Nature* (London and New York: Routledge, 1991), 149.
18. Ibid., 191–92.
19. Ibid., 193.
20. Ibid., 175.
21. Ibid., 176.
22. Homi K. Bhabha, *The Location of Culture* (London and New York: Routledge, 1994), 254.
23. Ibid., 254.
24. Toni Morrison, *Beloved* (New York: Alfred A. Knopf, 1987), 256–57.

Killing Rage

1. Original text.
2. Cornel West, *Race Matters* (New York: Vintage Books, 1994), 136.
3. bell hooks, *Killing Rage: Ending Racism* (New York: Henry Hol and Company, 1995), 13.
4. *Race Matters,* 28.
5. bell hooks, *Killing Rage*, 248–50.
6. Toni Morrison, *Sula* (New York: A Plume/Penquin Book, 1982), 118–19.
7. Cornel West, *Race Matters*, 150–51.
8. bell hooks, *Killing Rage*, 203.

Outlandishness

1. Translator's translation.
2. Sara Suleri, *The Rhetoric of English India,* in *The Post Colonial Studies Reader,* edited by Bill Ashcroft, Gareth Griffiths, Helen Tiffen (London and New York: Routledge, 1995), 112–13.
3. Trinh T. Minh-ha, *When the Moon Waxes Red: Representation, Gender, and Cultural Politics* (New York and London: Routledge, 1991), 180–81.
4. Gayatri Chakravorty Spivak, *Can the Subaltern Speak?,* in *Marxism and the Interpre-*

tation of Culture, edited by Cary Nelson and Lawrence Grosberg, (London: Macmillan, 1988), 74.

5. Homi Bhabha, *Signs taken for Wonders: Questions of Ambivalence and Authority Under a Tree Outside Dehli, May 1817,* in *Europe and Its Others,* edited by Francis Barker et al. vol. 1, 493.

6. Edward Kamau Braithwaite, *Creolization in Jamaica,* in *The Post Colonial Studies Reader,* edited by Bill Ashcroft, Gareth Griffiths, and Helen Tiffen (London and New York: Routledge, 1995), 205.

7. Anita Desai, *Baumgartner's Bombay* (London: Penguin Books, 1988), 20.

8. Ibid., 111.

Irony

1. Original text.

2. Donna Haraway, *Simians, Cyborgs and Women,* 149.

3. Salman Rushdie, *The Moor's Last Sigh* (New York: Pantheon Books, 1995), 301.

4. Ibid., 266

5. Hakim Bey, *T.A.Z. The Temporary Autonomous Zone: Ontological Anarchy, Poetic Terrorism* (New York: Autonomedia, 1991), 128.

6. Maurizio Viano, *Droghe, psichismi cyber e Punk,* in *Cibernauti. Tecnologia, comunicazione, democrazia: Elementi di psiconautica,* edited by Franco Berardi (Bifo), (Interventi del convegno organizzato dal Consorzio Università-Città di Bologna 16–17 June 1994) (Roma: Castelvecchi, 1994), 71.

7. Hakim Bey, T. A. Z., 119.

8. Paola Bora, *Il popolo Licio nel "Moeurs des sauvages americains" di J. F. Lafitau. Proposte di lettura per un rapporto fra J.J. Bachofen e la cultura settecentesca*", in "*Annali della Scuola Normale superiore di Pisa*" (Pisa, 1988), series 3, vol. 18, no. 2: 809.

9. Gerald Vizenor, *Manifest Manners: Postindian Warriors of Survivance* (Hannover and London: Wesleyan University Press, 1994), 89.

10. Ibid., 17.

Betraying Your Origins

1. The importance of the concept of passing has in the pedagogic field is the subject of an article by Pamela Caughie, *Not Entirely Strange . . . not Entirely Friendly: Passing and Pedagogy* in "*College English,*" vol. 54, no. 7 (November 1992), 775–93.

2. Franco Berardi (Bifo), *Neuromagma. Lavaro cognito e infoproduzione* (Rome: Costelvecchi, 1995), 203.

3. In this regard, see *"Let It Pass: Changing the Subject, Once Again," PMLA* (January 1997), by Pamela Caughie, where the author discusses how the displacement of the feminist subject within the poststructuralist paradigm undermines at the roots the identity of all women.

4. The processes of *deterritorialization* and *reterrorialization* are explained by Gilles Deleuze and Felix Guattari: "We need to see how everyone, at every age, in the smallest

things as in the greatest challenges, seeks a territory, tolerates or carries out deterritorialization, and is reterritorialized on almost anything—memory, fetish, or dream. . . . We cannot even say what comes first, and perhaps every territory presupposes a prior deterritorialization, or every thing happens at the same time . . . The merchant buys in a territory, deterritorializes products into commodities, and is territorialized on commercial circuits. In capitalism, capital or property is deterritorialized, ceases to be landed, and is reterritorialized on the means of production; whereas labor becomes 'abstract' labor, reterritorialized in wages; this is why Marx not only speaks of capital and labor but feels the need to draw up some true psychosocial types, both antipathetic and sympathetic: *the* capitalist and *the* proletarian." Gilles Deleuze and Felix Guattari, *What is Philosophy?* (New York: Columbia University Press, 1994), 67–68.

5. Nella Larson, *Passing* (New York: Negro Universities Press, 1969), 36–37.
6. Ibid., 90.
7. Ibid., 95.
8. Ibid., 97–98.
9. Ibid., 181.
10. Ibid., 199–201.

Rerun the Memory

1. Franco Berardi (Bifo), *Neuromagma,* 147.
2. Norbert Wiener, *Cybernetics: or Control and Communication in the Animal and the Machine* (Cambridge, MA: M.I.T. Press, 1994), 121.
3. Ibid., 11.
4. Ibid., 121.
5. Ibid., 124.
6. Lea Melandri, *Lo strabismo della memoria* (Milan: La Tartaruga, 1991), 16.
7. Alain Finkielkraut, *Le juif imaginaire* (Paris: Gallimard, 1980).
8. Pierre Lévy, *L'intelligence collective* (Paris: Gallimard, 1994).

Trespassing the Borders

1. Luce Irigaray, *Io tu noi* (Turin: Bollati Boringhieri, 1992), 41.
2. Ibid., 18.
3. Donna Haraway, *Simians, Cyborgs, and Women,* 208–12.
4. Ibid., 208.
5. Mario Perniola, *Il sex-appeal dell'inorganico* (Turin: Einaudi, 1994), 66.
6. Emily Prager, *Eve's Tattoo,* New York, Vintage Contemporaries, 1992.
7. Mario Perniola, *Il sex-appeal,* 13, (emphasis mine).
8. Ibid., 92.
9. Arthur and Marilouise Kroker, eds., *The Last Sex: Feminism and Outlaw Bodies* (New York: St. Martins Press, 1993).
10. Ibid., 51.

11. Helèna Velena, *Dal cybersex al transgender: Tecnologie, identità e politiche di liberazione* (Rome: Castelvecchi, 1995), 197.

Passing

1. Michael White and David Epston, *Narrative Means to Therapeutic Ends* (New York and London: W. W. Norton & Company, 1990), 36–37.
2. Hakim Bey, T. A. Z.
3. Laurie Anderson, "The Ugly One with the Jewels." Warner Bros., Records Inc., 1995 (from the book *Stories from the Nerve Bible* [New York: Harper Collins Publishers, 1994]).

Bibliography

Acker, Kathy. 1993. Against the Ordinary Language: The Language of the Body. In *The Last Sex: Feminism and Outlaw Bodies,* edited by Author and Marilouise Kroker. New York: St. Martins Press.

Anderson, Laurie. 1994. *Stories from the Nerve Bible.* New York: Harper Collins Publishers.

Anzieu, Didier. 1985. *Le Moi Peau.* Paris: Dunod.

Appadurai, Arjun. 1986. *The Social life of Things. Commodities in Cultural Perspective:* Cambridge, Cambridge University Press.

Arendt, Hannah. 1958. *The Human Condition.* Chicago: The University of Chicago Press.

———. 1961. *Between Past and Future: Eight Exercises in Political Thought.* New York: Viking Press.

———. 1963. *On Revolution.* New York: Viking Press.

———. 1978 *The Life of the Mind.* Edited by Mary Mc Carthy. New York: Harcourt Brace Jovanovich.

Bhabha, Homi. 1985. "Signs taken for Wonders: Questions of Ambivalence and Authority under a Tree Outside Dehli, May 1817." In *Europe and Its Others,* edited by Francis Barker et al. vol. 1. Colchester: University of Essex.

———. 1994. *The Location of Culture.* London and New York: Routledge.

Baudrillard, Jean (1992. *L'illusion de la fin, la greve des evenements, Paris, Galilee*

Benjamin, Walter. 1968. Illuminations. New York: Schocken.

Berardi, Franco (Bifo). 1995. *Neuromagma: Lavoro cognitivo e infoproduzione.* Rome: Castelvecchi.

Bey, Hakim. 1991. *T.A.Z. The Temporary Autonomous Zone: Ontological Anarchy, Poetic Terrorism.* New York: Autonomedia.

Bora, Paola. 1988. "Il popolo Licio nel 'Moeurs des sauvages americains' di J. F. Lafitau. Proposte di lettura per un rapporto fra J. J. Bachofen e la cultura settecentesca," in "*Annali della Scuola Normale superiore di Pisa.*" Pis, (Italy). Series 3, vol. 18, no. 2: 809.

Bordieau, Pierre. 1984. *Distinction: A Social Critique of the Judgement of Taste.* Cambridge, MA: Harvard University Press.

Braidotti, Rosi. 1994. *Nomadic Subjects: Embodiment and Sexual Difference in Contemporary Feminist Theory.* New York: Columbia University Press.

Braithwaite Kamau, Edward. 1995. "Creolization in Jamaica." In *The Post Colonial Studies Reader,* edited by Bill Ashcroft, Gareth Griffiths, and Helen Triffen. London and New York: Routledge.

Butler, Judith. 1990. *Gender Trouble: Feminism and the Subversion of Identity.* New York: Routledge.

Caughie, Pamela. 1991. "Let It Pass: Changing the Subject, Once Again" in *PMLA* (January).

———. 1992. "Not Entirely Strange . . . not Entirely Friendly: Passing and Pedagogy" in *College English,* vol. 54, no.7, (November).

Cixous, Helen. 1993. *Three Steps on the Ladder of Writing.* New York: Columbia University Press.

Debord, Guy. 1977. *The Society of the Spectacle.* London: Black and Red.

Descartes, Renee. 1988. *Selected Philosophical Writings.* Edited by J. Cottingham, R. Stoodhoff and P.Duro. Cambridge: Cambridge University Press.

De Certeau, Michel. 1984. *The Practice of Everyday Life.* Berkeley and L.A.: University of California Press.

De Lauretis, Teresa. 1987. *Technologies of Gender.* Bloomington: Indiana University Press.

Deleuze, Gilles and Felix Guattari. 1983. *Anti-Oedipus:Capitalism and Schizophrenia.* Minneapolis: University of Minnesota Press.

———. 1987. *A Thousand Plateaus.* Minneapolis: University of Minnesota Press.

Desai, Anita. 1988. *Baumgartner's Bombay.* London: Penguin Books.

Diotima Group. 1987. *Il pensiero della differenza sessuale.* Milano: La Tartaruga.

———. 1990. *Mettere al mondo il mondo.* Milano: La Tartaruga.

———. 1995 *Oltre l'uguaglianza.* Genoa, Italy, Liguori.

Du Bois, W. E. 1969. *The Souls of Black Folk.* New York: Signet Classics.

Fanon, Frantz. 1967. *The Wretched of the Earth.* Harmondsworth: Penguin.

———. 1986. *Black Skin, White Masks.* London: Pluto.

Finkielkraut, Alain. 1980. *Le juif imaginaire.* Paris: Gallimard.

Foucault, Michel. 1970. *The Order of Things.* London: Tavistock.

———. 1977. *Discipline and Punish: The Birth of Prison.* Harmondsworth: Penguin.

Freud, Sigmund. 1974. "The 'uncanny.'" Edited by J. Strahey. standard ed., 17. London: The Hogart Press.

Gargani, Aldo, ed. 1979. *Crisi della ragione.* Turin: Einaudi.

Gibson, William. 1984. *Neuromancer* London: Harper & Collins Science Fiction & Fantasy.

Gilroy, Paul. 1993. *The Black Atlantic: Modernity and Double-Consciousness.* Cambridge, MA: Harvard University Press.

Haraway, Donna. 1991. *Simians, Cyborgs, and Women.* New York: Routledge.

Hall, Stuart. 1990. "Cultural Studies and its Legacies." In *Cultural Studies,* edited by L. Grossberg et al. New York: Routledge.

Hebdige, Dick. 1979. *Subculture: The Meaning of Style.* London: Methuen.

Hegel, Georg W. F. 1929. *Science of Logic.* 2 vols., New York: Mac Millan Company.

———. 1977. *Phenomenolgy of Spirit.* New York: Oxford University Press.

hooks, bell. 1995. *Killing Rage: Ending Racism.* New York: Henry Hol and Company.

Hutcheon, Linda. 1989. *The Politics of Postmodernism.* London: Routledge.

Irigaray, Luce. 1985. *The Sex Which Is not One.* Ithaca, NY: Cornell University Press.

———. 1992. *Io tu noi.* Turin: Bollati Boringhieri.

Jameson Fredrich. 1991. *Postmodernism or the Cultural Logic of Late Capitalism.* Durham: Duke University Press.

Kant, Immanuel. 1957. *Perpetual Peace.* Upper Saddie River, NJ: Prenctice Hall.

———. 1970. *Political Writings.* Cambridge: Cambridge University Press.

———. 1995. *Foundation of the Metaphysicis of Moral & What is Enlightment?* Upper Saddie River, NJ: Prenctice Hall.

King, M. L. Jr. 1965. *The Civil Right Struggle In United States Today: An Address Delivered at the House of the Association (of the Bar the City of N.Y.).* New York: The Association.

———. 1967. *Conscience for Change.* Toronto: Canadian Broadcasting Company.

Kroker, Arthur and Marilouise, eds. 1993. *The Last Sex: Fminism and Otlaw Bodies.* New York: St. Martins Press.

Larson, Nella. 1969. *Passing.* New York: Negro Universities Press.

Latour, Bruno. 1987. *Science In Action: How to Follow Scientists and Engineers Through Society.* Cambridege, MA: Harvard University Press.

———. 1993. *We have Never Been Modern.* Cambridge, MA: Harvard University Press.

Lerner, Michael and Cornell West. 1995. *Jews and Blacks: Let the Healing Begin.* New York: HarperCollins.

Levy, Pierre. 1994. *L'intelligence collective.* Paris: Gallimard.

Levy-Strauss. 1976. *Tristes Tropique.* London: Penguin.

Lonzi, Carla. 1974. *Sputiamo su Hegel.* Milan: Scritti di Rivolta Femminile.

Lorde, Audre.' 1984. *Sister Outsider: Essays and Speeeches.* Trumansburg, NY: The Crossing Press.

Lyotard, Jean-Francois. 1988. *The Postmodern Condition: A Report on Knowledge.* Minneapolis: University of Minnesota Press.

Malcom X, 1992. *By Any Means Necessary.* New York: Pathfinder Press.

Maraini, Dacia. 1993. *Cercando Emma.* Milan: Rizzoli.

Marx, Karl. 1946. *Capital.* London: J. P. Dent.

———. 1973. *Grundrisse. Foundation of the Critique of Political Economy.* New York: Random House.

Melandri, Lea. 1991. *Lo strabismo della memoria.* Milan: La Tartaruga.

Mohanti, Chandra. 1991. "Under Western Eyes: Feminist scholarship and Colonial Discourse." In *Third World Women and the Politics of Feminism,* edited by Mohanti Chandra, Ann Russo, and Lourdes Torres. Indianapolis: Indiana University Press.

Morrison, Toni. 1982. *Sula.* New York: APlume/Penguin Book.

———. 1987. *Beloved.* London: Chatto & Windus.

Mudimbe, V. Y. 1988. *The Invention of Africa: Gnosis, Philosophy, and the Order of Knowledge.* Bloomington: Indiana University Press.

Mukerjee, Bharati. 1993. *Holder of the World.* New York: Knopf.

Mulvey, Laura. 1989. *Visual and Other Pleasures.* Bloomington: Indiana University Press.

Muraro, Luisa. 1991. *L'ordine simbolico della madre.* Rome: Editori Riuniti.

Naipaul V. S. 1981. *Among the Believers: An Islamic Journey.* London: Deutsch.

———. 1986. *Away in the World.* London: Heineman.

Perniola, Mario. 1994. *Il sex-appeal dell'inorganico.* Turin: Einaudi.

Prager, Emily. 1992. *Eve's Tattoo.* New York: Vintage Contemporaries.

Rushdie, Salman. 1988. *The Satanic Verses.* London: Viking.

———. 1995. *The Moor's Last Sigh.* New York: Pantheon Books, *Est, West,* New York, Pantheon Press.

Sahlins, Marshall. 1976. *Culture and Practical Reason.* Chicago: Chicago University Press.

Said, Edward. 1978. *Orientalism.* London: Routledge.

Shelley, Mary. 1987. *Mary Shelley's Frankenstein.* New York: Chelsea Publisher.

Shoat, Ella, and Robert Stam. 1994. *Unthinking Eurocentrism: Multiculturalism and the Media.* London: Routledge.

Sylvester, Robert. 1995. *A Celebration of Neurons: An Educator's Guide to the Human Brain.* Alexandria, VA: ASCD.

Spivak Chakravorty, Gayatri. 1988. "Can the Subaltern Speak?" in *Marxism and the Interpretation of Culture,* edited by Cary Nelson and Laurence Grossberg. London: Macmillan.

Suleri, Sara. 1992. *The Rethoric of English India.* Chicago: Chicago University Press.

Trinh T. Minh-ha. 1991. *When the Moon Waxes Red: Representation, Gender, and Cultural Politics.* New York and London: Routledge.

Velena, Helèna. 1995. *Dal cybersex al transgender: Tecnologie, identità e politiche di liberazi*one. Rome: Castelvecchi.

Velie, Alan. 1982. *Four American Indian Masters.* Norman: University of Oklaoma Press.

Viano, Maurizio. 1994. "Droghe, psichismi cyber e punk." In *Cibernauti: Tecnologia, comunicazione, democrazia. Elementi di psiconautica* (Interventi del convegno organizzato dal Consorzio Università- Città di Bologna June 16–17, 1994), edited by Franco Berardi (Bifo). Rome: Castelvecchi.

Vizenor, Gerald. 1994. *Manifest Manners: Poetindian Warriors of Survivance.* Hannover and London: Wesleyan University Press.

West, Cornel. 1995. *Race Matters.* New York: Vintage Books.

White, Michael and David Epston. 1990. *Narrative Means to Therapeutic Ends.* New York and London: W. W. Norton & Company.

Wiener, Norbert. 1994. *Cybernetics: Or Control and Communication in the Animal and the Machine.* Cambridge, MA: M.I.T. Press.

Wilde Oscar. 1992. *The Picture of Dorian Gray.* New York: Random House.

Wittig, Monique. 1973. *Les Guerrilleres.* New York: Avon.

Index

Date Due →

2/12/08		

Books returned after due date are subject to a fine.